Series Editor:
Paul Wehman, Ph.D.

Th
Tra......
Adulthood Series

TEACHING TRANSITION SKILLS IN
Inclusive Schools

The Brookes
Transition to
Adulthood Series

TEACHING
TRANSITION SKILLS IN
Inclusive Schools

by

Teresa Grossi, Ph.D.

and

Cassandra M. Cole, Ed.D.

Indiana Institute on Disability and Community
Indiana University
Bloomington

·P·A·U·L·H·
BROOKES
PUBLISHING CO.®

Baltimore • London • Sydney

·P A U L·H·
BRŒKES
PUBLISHING C?.®

Paul H. Brookes Publishing Co.
Post Office Box 10624
Baltimore, Maryland 21285-0624
USA

www.brookespublishing.com

Typeset by Scribe, Philadelphia, Pennsylvania.
Manufactured in the United States of America by
Bradford & Bigelow, Newburyport, Massachusetts.

The individuals described in this book are composites or real people whose situations are masked and are based on the authors' actual experiences. Real names and identifying details are used by permission.

Library of Congress Cataloging-in-Publication Data

Grossi, Teresa (Teresa Ann), author.
 Teaching transition skills in inclusive schools / by Teresa Grossi, Ph.D. and Cassandra
M. Cole, Ed.D.
  pages   cm.   – (The Brookes transition to adulthood series)
 Includes bibliographical references and index.
 ISBN 978-1-59857-233-9 (pbk. : alk. paper)
 ISBN 1-59857-233-4 (pbk. : alk. paper)
1. Students with disabilities–Education (Secondary)–United States. 2. Students with disabilities–Vocational guidance–
United States. 3. High school students–Vocational guidance–United States. 4. School-to-work transition–United
States. 5. Inclusive education–United States. I. Cole, Cassandra M., author. II. Title.
LC4031.G687 2013
371.9'0473–dc23   2012045861

British Library Cataloguing in Publication data are available from the British Library.

2017   2016   2015   2014   2013

10   9   8   7   6   5   4   3   2   1

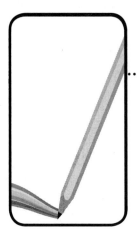

Contents

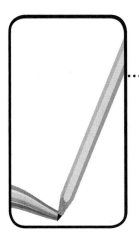

Series Preface

The Brookes Transition to Adulthood Series was developed for the purpose of meeting the critical educational needs of students with disabilities who will be moving from school to adulthood. It is no longer acceptable to simply equip a student with a set of isolated life skills that may or may not be relevant to his or her adult life. Nor is it sufficient to treat the student as if he or she will remain unchanged throughout life. As we allow for growth and change in real-life environments, so must we allow for growth and change in the individuals who will operate within the environments. Today, transition must concern itself with the whole life pattern of each student as it relates to his or her future. However, integrating the two constructs of self and the real adult world for one student at a time is not always straightforward. It requires skills and knowledge. It requires a well-thought-out, well-orchestrated team effort. It takes individualization, ingenuity, perseverance, and more.

The results of these first-rate efforts can be seen when they culminate in a student with a disability who exits school prepared to move to his or her life beyond the classroom. Unfortunately, though, this does not always happen. This is because transition has become a splintered concept, too weighted down by process and removed from building on the student's aspirations and desires for "a good life." However, it does not have to be this way.

This book series is designed to help the teachers, transition specialists, rehabilitation counselors, community service providers, administrators, policy makers, other professionals, and families who are looking for useful information on a daily basis by translating the evidence-based transition research into practice. Each volume addresses specific objectives that are related to the all-important and overarching goal of helping students meet the demands of school and society and gain a greater understanding of themselves so that they are equipped for success in the adult world.

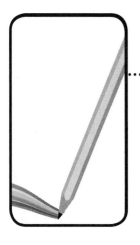

Editorial Advisory Board

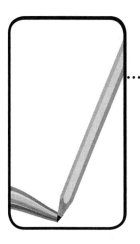

About the Authors

Teresa Grossi, Ph.D., is Director of the Center on Community Living and Careers at the Indiana Institute on Disability and Community at Indiana University. The Center's work focuses on secondary transition services and employment and adult services through partnerships with schools, state agencies, and support organizations. Dr. Grossi has extensive experience working in schools and with adult employment providers. She is a faculty member at Indiana University's School of Education where she teaches transition courses and has conducted research and written on secondary transition services, community supports, and employment issues for individuals with disabilities. In addition, Dr. Grossi has conducted program evaluations for school districts and other state and national programs. She has directed numerous federal and state grant projects. Currently, Dr. Grossi serves as the external evaluator for the National Secondary Transition and Technical Assistance Center.

Cassandra (Sandi) Cole, Ed.D., is Director of the Center on Education and Lifelong Learning at the Indiana Institute on Disability and Community at Indiana University. Prior to joining the university, Sandi spent 22 years as a public school teacher and administrator at both the elementary and secondary levels. Her areas of expertise include collaboration, teacher leadership, school change and redesign, teacher appraisal systems, school-wide discipline, and instructional practices for diverse learners. In addition, Dr. Cole has conducted numerous program evaluations for schools districts and directed large-scale federal and state grant projects. Dr. Cole is a faculty member in the Indiana University Graduate School and directs the Special Education Leadership program in the Indiana University School of Education. Dr. Cole has consulted extensively with school districts across the country on designing schools that are inclusive of all students. Her research includes a large-scale study of student achievement.

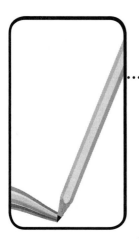

Preface

Over the years as we have worked in schools around inclusive practices and secondary transition services, we have been frustrated with the "separateness" of transition and instructional practices in special education. We continually found ourselves speaking to both general and special educators to show how good instructional practices and structures in the general education system improve postsecondary outcomes for *all* students. In schools where we found good instructional practices in the general education environment, we found many practices and activities that were applicable to inform the transition planning process for students with disabilities, but the special educators were not necessarily aware of them. Many times when we would relate this information to the special educators, they would have those "aha!" moments.

In addition, we have spent a good portion of our careers working in schools and districts to merge the general and special education systems into a unified system of service delivery. We felt that the unified system concept was applicable to secondary transition services and planning for all students, with some unique aspects for students with disabilities.

The conceptual framework for this book has been based on our work and lessons learned over the years. Although the focus of this book is on students with mild disabilities, it can be applicable to many students. This book is designed to help all classroom teachers, transition personnel, and administrators to see the possibilities within their own district of transition services for all students. It is our hope that all students, especially students with disabilities, leave school prepared for college and careers.

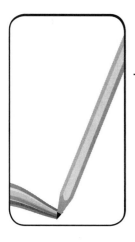

Acknowledgments

We would like to acknowledge our colleagues at the Center on Community Living and Careers and the Center On Education and Lifelong Learning at the Indiana Institute on Disability and Community who continuously inform our work. They are a dedicated, caring, and committed group of professionals who have influenced our work and the lives of countless number of young adults and adults with disabilities and educators. Specifically, we would like to thank Barbara Horvath, whose work informed various sections of this book. Barb's passion and expertise in differentiated instruction and universal design for learning has made learning accessible for all.

We would also like to thank *The Brookes Transition to Adulthood Series* editor and Editorial Advisory Board for their comments, suggestions, and guidance. Specifically, we need to thank Paul Wehman for inviting us to be a part of this series, and Rebecca Lazo, Senior Acquisitions Editor, and Steve Plocher, Associate Editor, for their feedback and brainstorming time for the organization of this book.

In memory of our mothers . . . who believed in us, guided us, and taught us to reach for the stars. Their spirit lives within us.

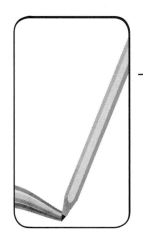

1

Expanding Our Thinking About High Schools

A Unified Framework for Secondary Transition Services

Today's high schools are charged with preparing students for college and careers. This may not sound new; however, preparing all students for life after high school has changed drastically from even a generation ago.

The workforce of the future will be more highly educated, and students will be part of a global workforce and society. Current data indicate that

- An estimated 60% of jobs in America will require some postsecondary education by 2018 (Center on Education and the Workforce, 2010)

- Over the next 25 years nearly half of the projected job growth will be in occupations that require higher education and skill levels (Wagner, 2008)

> *The Obama Administration has set a goal for the U.S. to have the best educated workforce and highest proportion of college graduates by 2020 asking all Americans to commit to taking at least one year of higher education or career training after high school.*
>
> *—Obama, 2009*

For the past three decades, many leaders have realized the urgency to create high schools that give students the skills, habits, and confidence to be successful in the global workplace. The education field has known for years that to effectively guide students toward necessary higher education and career preparation, high schools must be more student centered with greater personalized programs, support services, and meaningful instruction that connect students to their passions, interests, and learning preferences.

Despite the widely recognized need for change, many high schools have continued to operate and function in the same way that they did 50 or more years ago. Progress can be paralyzed by the day-to-day challenges that high schools face, such as high-stakes testing and increased accountability, limited resources, increasing student body size, diversity of student populations, increased external pressures (e.g., business, government, private sector), the fast pace of technology, students who have intensive behavior and health needs, lack of community and parent involvement, changes in administrative leadership, and bureaucratic structures.

However, there are models of successful and innovative high schools. The field relies heavily on Ernest Boyer's work *High School: A Report on Secondary Education in America* (1983); Ted Sizer's *Horace's Compromise* (1984); *A Nation at Risk* (National Commission on Excellence and Education, 1983); and *Breaking Ranks II* (for which Sizer wrote the foreword; 2004), which provides a comprehensive, practical report on how high schools might better meet the needs of all students. All of these early works call for

- Greater personalization
- Increased rigor
- Student-driven, inquiry-based learning
- Self-reflection
- Instruction based on student interests
- Development of students' mind and character
- Collaborative structures
- Critical thinking and problem solving
- Smaller units of learning (learning communities)
- Interdisciplinary teams
- Continuous program improvement
- Inclusive practices

INCLUSION OF STUDENTS WITH DISABILITIES IN HIGH SCHOOLS

Rethinking high schools has a large impact on students with disabilities. Like other students, those with disabilities struggle with the traditional approaches to instruction. One of the key challenges facing students with disabilities is having access to full participation in postsecondary education and employment (National Center on Secondary Education and Transition, 2003, p. 1). Students with disabilities participating in postsecondary education continue to increase, from 31% in 2003 to 55% in 2009 (Newman, Wagner, Cameto, Knokey, and Shaver, 2010), but still lag behind their peers without disabilities. As requirements for success after high school increase, it is even more urgent to look at changes in high schools that better support all students so that they can access postsecondary training and education.

 **Myisha and Brad**

Myisha is a high school junior who has been provided support for her education through an individualized education program (IEP). Prior to entering high school, Myisha had opportunities through elementary and middle school to be educated with her peers: She was a full member of her general education classrooms, where she received adaptations and modifications that enabled her to have full access to the core curriculum. She sometimes received additional support from a learning specialist who supplemented her program for reading and taught her strategies to manage anxiety. In middle school, Myisha participated in the Reality Store, a simulation in which students choose careers, make decisions about their budgets and lifestyles, and then review and assess their decisions and financial status. Like all her friends in high school, when Myisha was a freshman, she took an assessment to understand her learning style and strengths and completed a graduation plan that included a career interest inventory. In her second semester English class's career unit, she researched her top two careers and wrote about the careers and their requirements, as well as how to use online resources. In her sophomore year, Myisha toured the Career-Tech Center (i.e., Career Technical Center or Vocational Education Center), which specializes in vocational education, to explore potential careers in her interest areas of nursing and health careers. She also completed a self-determination assessment with her resource teacher to help with decision making and understanding her accommodation needs. Now as a junior, Myisha is working hard to keep up her GPA by using her reading comprehension learning strategies in her content classes and applying self-advocacy skills by voicing her accommodation needs to her teachers. Although she chose not to attend the Career-Tech Center to complete the health care career pathway courses, she is looking forward to attending the college and career nights at the high school next semester. Her goal is to study nursing in college. She is looking forward to sharing an apartment with her best friend and being on her own.

Brad is also a high school junior who has had an IEP since his early education years. He struggles with attention, organization, and study skills and often has difficulty engaging with his peers. He is a strong visual learner and notices small details. He loves hands-on activities and does well in science. Prior to entering high school, Brad was assigned to general education homerooms and was pulled out to a special education classroom for services in reading and math. Throughout middle school, Brad continued to receive pull-out services during language arts and math periods. As he entered high school, his IEP team decided Brad probably would not pursue postsecondary education, and so Brad was enrolled in self-contained special education content classes. Based on a career interest inventory and his father's influence, Brad had a strong interest in cars and hands-on activities. In his sophomore year, he toured the Career-Tech Center to explore the options of enrolling in auto mechanics. He also completed a self-determination assessment with his resource teacher to help with goal setting and understanding his accommodation needs. Like Myisha, he participated in the Reality Store simulation. It was during this experience that Brad knew he wanted to work on cars. The transition coordinator identified possible community sites where Brad could get work experience, perhaps even paid. Brad's dream is to one day own a repair shop.

It is clear that Brad and Myisha had similar abilities and goals. However, access and expectations differed for Brad. His experiences from elementary to high school were primarily associated with special education services rather than with experiencing the general education environment. Access to the general education environment would have provided him with access to a broader curriculum, higher expectations, and possibly a different career path.

A study of postsecondary outcomes of students with mild disabilities across inclusive and noninclusive settings found that students in inclusive settings

- Had greater access to the general education curriculum

- Had higher rates for passing the state proficiency test

- Had higher expectations and were more involved in extracurricular activities

- Had higher graduation rates and improved postschool outcomes (Grossi & Cole, 2007)

Transition services looked different in the two settings: Students in inclusive high schools participated in many transition activities that were available to all students, such as interest inventories and career planning, often led by the guidance counselor. Students in noninclusive settings engaged in transition activities that were often separate and led by the special education teacher, with limited access to the rich information that other students received. As students in inclusive settings moved through high school, these general transition services were supplemented with additional resources for their unique needs, such as vocational rehabilitation services, connection to college services for students with disabilities, and mental health supports. Not surprisingly, outcomes were best for students who spent time in inclusive settings from preschool through high school. The Grossi and Cole (2007) study and others such as the National Longitudinal Transition Study-2 (NLTS-2) highlight that quality transition outcomes are dependent on excellent educational systems—systems that are unified and that provide all students with access to high quality curriculum and instruction, flexible structures, and a culture of caring and personalization.

Over the years, the movement toward including students with disabilities in general education programs has significantly changed the way these students access education. Yet, many students with disabilities continue to move through high schools in a parallel track, with separate classrooms, separate curriculum, and separate transition services and activities. These students, like Brad, are not a part of the general education classroom and miss the full experience of extracurricular activities and graduation planning that is essential for positive postsecondary outcomes. For these students, transition planning is often an event that takes place in isolation, rather than in conjunction with the kinds of activities that can be embedded into classroom instruction and typical high school experiences. However, since the Individuals with Disabilities Education Act (IDEA) of 1990 (PL 101-476) and its amendments of 1997 (PL 105-17) mandate both that instruction should occur in the least restrictive environment and that transition planning must be part of adolescents' IEPs, transition planning must be a unified part of a student's high school experience, rather than a separate system.

There are recommended, promising, evidence-based practices for transition education and service provision that support the broad categories of student development, student-focused planning, interagency collaboration, family involvement, and program structures and attributes (Kohler, 1998; National Secondary Transition Technical Assistance Center [NSTTAC], 2008). In addition, there are recommended courses and assessments for graduation (e.g., state graduation requirements, state proficiency tests, Common Core State Standards initiative) and recommended reforms to improve high schools (Sizer, 2004b; *Breaking Ranks II*, 2004). The challenge for educators is to combine these efforts. Students receiving special education services are required to meet rigorous education standards, but their transition needs also should be met—both to meet the requirements of the law and to ensure positive postschool outcomes. This is most possible when students have access to high expectations, quality instruction, general education experiences, and personalization.

The push and pull of school change is strong; while there is a strong push from all segments of society for changing how high schools do business, the pull to continue doing school as usual can be equally strong. However, as curricula are now being revised in many states to align with the Common Core State Standards (see http://www.corestandards .org/), new opportunities exist to ensure that students with disabilities have access to the environments that prepare them for college and careers.

A UNIFIED FRAMEWORK FOR SECONDARY TRANSITION SERVICES

The following conceptual framework outlined is based on a set of our guiding principles for educating all students.

1. All students have the right to meaningful participation in the core curriculum with their neighborhood peers.

2. Transition planning and services should be provided within a unified system of supports for all students.

3. A culture of collaboration among students, families, administrators, and staff is essential for transition planning.

4. Special education services should supplement rather than supplant core curriculum.

5. A student's education must consider academic, social, and emotional learning.

6. Knowledge and understanding of a student's culture must be considered in a child's education and preparation for future environments.

Expanding on the work of Kochhar-Bryant and Bassett (2003) and Kochhar-Bryant and Greene (2009), in a unified framework, transition services are an integrated, cohesive process that provides experiences to prepare *all* students for college, careers, and citizenship. IDEA's requirements established a much-needed service for students with disabilities, but it has been operationalized and practiced as something unique for students with disabilities. If, in fact, students are to be prepared for college, careers, and citizenship, then all students need individualized transition education and planning and access to the necessary services and activities.

Figure 1.1 illustrates the conceptual framework for a unified framework for delivering secondary transition education and services. At the center are the components that

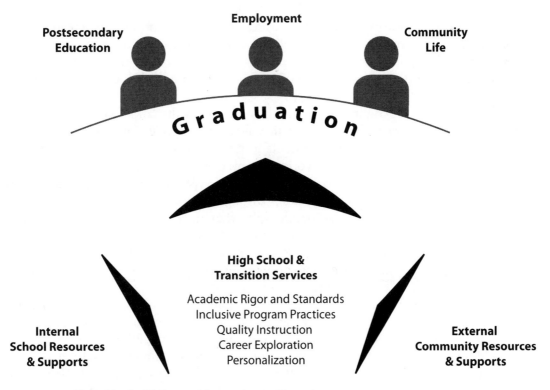

Figure 1.1. A unified framework for secondary transition services.

ensure a solid foundation for positive postsecondary outcomes for all students. Access to quality instruction, academic rigor and standards, personalization, career exploration, and inclusive practices should begin in the early elementary years and continue through to graduation. The components are interrelated, and as students move toward graduation, each component helps them to narrow and define their postschool goals.

A school that provides high-quality instruction ensures that staff use a variety of instructional strategies and assessments to accommodate individual learning styles. Educators have the knowledge and skills to design rigorous units of study that respect learner differences and apply the principles of differentiation to ensure that all students succeed in meaningful, appropriately challenging learning experiences (Tomlinson & McTighe, 2006). Instructional design reduces barriers to access by utilizing universal design for learning (UDL), which provides multiple means of representation, expression, and engagement for all learners (Rose & Meyer, 2002). Teachers intentionally gather information from students and families to understand student readiness, interests, and learning profiles (Tomlinson, 1999). Quality instruction matched to a student's assessed entry skills increases student success, reduces behavioral difficulties, and avoids the need for special education evaluation and placement (Gravois, Knotek, & Babinski, 2002).

Academic rigor and standards must guide quality instruction to ensure that high expectations are not reserved for a few. The Common Core State Standards (National Governors Association Center for Best Practices and the Council of Chief State School Officers, 2010a) established the essential skills a student should master in order to graduate and be prepared for college or career. Positive postschool outcomes depend on the student's ability to access the standards, as well as adequate support to master them, and to apply knowledge and skills in the real world.

Personalization is also a key to academic success. Schools must create flexible structures (e.g., student schedules, school day, school year, advisories, organizational units) that provide students with opportunities to build meaningful relationships with adults and peers. It also requires that schools attend to the physical, social, and emotional needs of students.

In addition to rigor and personalization, McNulty and Quaglia (2007) added relevance as a necessary element of quality instruction. Relevant learning is interdisciplinary and contextual. It requires students to do authentic work and apply core knowledge, concepts, or skills to solve real-world, complex problems. Relevant learning involves the use of prior knowledge, the development of in-depth understanding, and the ability to develop and express ideas and findings through elaborated communication.

As students build their academic skills, they must have opportunities to apply them in a variety of settings, exploring the various careers that may match their strengths, preferences, and interests. Career exploration must be embedded in a student's high school life; teachers must facilitate career connections within their academic and extracurricular activities. Students should engage in a variety of career exploration activities, including career interest inventories, career assessments, and career units. Opportunities for internships, apprenticeships, job shadowing, and early college experiences are examples of ways students can explore careers in real-life contexts (Luecking, 2009).

Finally, a solid foundation for student success requires that school structures and culture support the inclusion of all students in the everyday fabric of the educational institution. There should be a shared responsibility among all staff to address cultural, behavioral, linguistic, and academic differences of students so that all groups benefit equally from instruction, classroom management, and transition practices.

Multiple Levels of Transition Services and Supports

The core components previously described continue to support student growth and learning as students move toward graduation. During their high school experience, all students should have opportunities to participate in transition activities that are universal, not unlike the first tier of universal supports that all students can access in a response to intervention (RTI) model (National Response to Intervention Center, 2012) or Multi-tier System of Support (MTSS) model. MTSS is a term that many states are embracing to include behavioral as well as academic supports for all students. Examples of universal supports would include four-year high school plans, career guidance and counseling, career nights, college nights, college visitations, career-tech programs (vocational education), service learning, career assessments, elective courses of interest that support transition goals, and so on. These services and activities are expanded throughout students' high school years and are refined as they near graduation.

However, some students will need additional services and supports to assist in their transitions through high school and beyond (e.g., a targeted group like Tier 2 in RTI). Figure 1.1 shows internal (school) and external (community) supports that can be accessed by students. While some of these supports may be unique for students with disabilities, many of them can and should be accessed by any student. All youth benefit from having a support system or network as they prepare to exit high school and enter college, work, or community life (Rennie Center for Education Research & Policy, 2011; Willis, 2008). It is important to note that these external and internal supports combine with the high school and transition services: They supplement, rather than supplant, transition services.

Internal supports are the services provided by individual schools or the school districts. For all students, these include school psychology services, guidance counseling programs, social worker support, and career planning. Specialized services include curricular accommodations and modifications, special education services, related services (e.g., speech-language pathology services, occupational and physical therapy services, assistive technology), school nursing services, suicide prevention and/or antibullying programs, and peer supports.

External supports are community resources that support students throughout high school and ensure graduation and postsecondary success. In addition to a student's personal community network, including neighbors, potential business contacts, and family and friends, there are specialized services for students requiring greater support. Often these services are provided through collaborative relationships with the schools and may include One-Stop Career Centers, business partnerships, health services, substance abuse and addiction services, family support services, social services (e.g., housing, food stamps), the juvenile justice system, and public transportation, as well as unique disability services from agencies such as Vocational Rehabilitation, Mental Health, Developmental Disabilities, and postsecondary education disability support services.

Students with higher support needs may require a more individualized or unique approach to academic instruction and transition planning. Again, this would be more aligned to the Tier 3 of the RTI model, and we will talk more about support for students with unique needs in Chapter 5.

The outcomes represented by the arrows at the top of the Figure 1.1 indicate the ultimate goals we encourage for all students, based on a collaborative, unified framework for secondary transition services.

SUMMARY

How high schools work and look affects the experiences, level of achievement, and post-school outcomes of students with and without disabilities. In the past, high schools have traditionally organized themselves and operated in ways that have marginalized students with disabilities and forced them into separate programs with different expectations. If the students with disabilities are to leave school to become productive citizens while furthering their education and training for a successful career or entering the work force, transition services must be unified and integrated with services and supports for all students.

If we were to apply the unified framework presented in this chapter to Myisha's and Brad's experiences, Myisha's education would be similar to what was described early in this chapter. Brad's experience, however, would look much different. At an early stage, he would have had access to the general education core curriculum and other inclusive school experiences with his peers. He would have had a variety of supports and services that enabled him to access the rigor of a high school curriculum without being pulled away from content teachers with the knowledge and skills to provide this rigor. His options upon entering high school would have been broader, and he may have been encouraged to go to a two- or four-year college to obtain the necessary skills to open his own business. He would have been afforded an opportunity to further explore his desire to open his own business by attending courses at the Career-Tech Center, while at the same time earning credits that would allow the opportunity for postsecondary education. His transition experiences would not have started with the transition coordinator, which supplanted the universal transition activities. Instead, the transition coordinator would have provided the supports, as needed, to facilitate his participation in the universal transition experiences (e.g., Career-Tech Center).

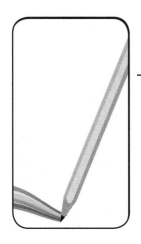

2

Good Transition Practices

Myisha and Brad

Both Myisha and Brad are starting their junior year in high school. Myisha has been working hard to keep up her GPA by using her reading comprehension learning strategies in her content classes and practicing her self-advocacy skills by requesting accommodation needs with her teachers. She is interested in exploring career opportunities in the health care professions and possibly studying nursing.

Brad's parents and teachers have learned that Brad needs an environment where he can move around. Brad has been working on using his coping strategies when he gets frustrated. He has a strong interest in cars and hands-on activities and has a dream of owning his own repair shop one day. Brad toured the Career-Tech Center to explore the options of enrolling in auto mechanics courses. The transition coordinator is working with Brad to participate in work experiences and helping him get a paid work experience.

Myisha and Brad are at a critical juncture in their high school experience. They, like all students, need appropriate services and supports to prepare them for postsecondary education, careers, and community life. These appropriate transition services and supports must be built upon over the years, helping the students define and redefine their postsecondary goals and ensure they are equipped with the proper strategies, accommodations, and supports to be successful in the future environments. This chapter will provide a brief overview of the transition planning process and practices and discuss the internal and external supports as well as the high school transition services shown in the graphic of the conceptual framework in Chapter 1 (for more in-depth information regarding individual transition planning and practices, please see *Essentials of Transition Planning* [Wehman, 2011]).

LEGISLATIVE INFLUENCE

It has been over two decades since the word *transition* was defined in law by IDEA 1990. IDEA 1990 provided the first formal definition of *transition* that required that the transition components of the IEP process be in place by the time the student reached the age of 16. It also included language on interagency collaboration. Subsequent amendments to IDEA in 1997 and 2004 (PL 108-446) continued to refine and expand the transition provisions for schools. An important change in the 1997 amendment was the emphasis of access, participation, and progress in the general education curriculum. As a result, special education had to be aligned with standards-based curriculum, and students with disabilities were required to participate in state and national assessments. The 1997 amendment added the requirement of transition services needs statement at the age of 14.

Changes in the 2004 IDEA reauthorization moved transition services from an outcome- to a results-oriented process. IDEA 2004 regulations were aligned with the No Child Left Behind Act of 2001 (PL 107-110) to assist schools in implementing these laws more seamlessly. IDEA 2004 defines transition services as "a coordinated set of activities for a child with a disability that [is] . . . designed to be within a results-oriented process, that is focused on improving the academic and functional achievement of the child with a disability to facilitate the child's movement from school to post school activities, including post-secondary education, vocational education, integrated employment (including supported employment), continuing and adult education, adult services, independent living, or community participation" (Section 602). Although IDEA 2004 returned to the age of 16 for addressing transition services needs (or younger if appropriate), many states continue to initiate transition planning at age 14. From these changes came a greater focus on accountability, and for transition services, this meant a focus on postschool outcomes.

QUALITY TRANSITION PRACTICES

A great deal of research and literature on quality transition practices has been presented to the field. In a review of both empirical and nonempirical publications, Greene (2009) identified a list of 12 recommended practices in transition. The most frequently cited transition practices include

1. Person-centered or student-focused planning

2. Parent or family involvement

3. Self-determination and self-advocacy

4. Integrated schools, classrooms, and employment

5. Career and vocational assessment and education

6. Community-based educational experiences

7. Postsecondary education participation and supports

8. Competitive paid work experiences in high school and beyond

9. Functional life-skills education

10. Social skills training and competency

11. Interagency collaboration and service coordination

12. Business and industry linkages with schools

Kohler (1998) introduced these practices as transition-focused education and provides a view of transition planning as a fundamental basis of education that guides the development of all educational programs. It is a shift from disability-focused deficit programs to an approach based on strengths, abilities, options, and self-determination. Kohler introduces the Taxonomy for Transition Programming as a comprehensive conceptual model of practices through which transition-focused education and services are developed and delivered. The Taxonomy for Transition Programming is one of the few models that is based on both empirical and validation studies. Her model is organized into five categories: student-focused planning, student development, family involvement, interagency collaboration, and program structures. This chapter will be organized around each of these five categories that include the practices described by other researchers as well (e.g., Greene, 2009; Deshler & Shumaker, 2006; Phelps & Hanley-Maxwell, 1997).

Often legislation is difficult to interpret and apply in practice. We have provided tables after each of the descriptions of the five categories of practice to connect legislation to practice (adapted from the NSTTAC's team planning tool, 2008).

Student-Focused Planning

Student-focused planning ensures that the student's goals, visions, strengths, and interests are central to the decision-making process in the development of the transition IEP. IDEA 2004 increased accountability by requiring states to develop a 6-year state performance plan (SPP) around 20 indicators on which data is submitted annually to the Office of Special Education Programs (OSEP). Individual student data are gathered by local school districts. Indicator 13 focuses on transition services:

> Percent of youth with IEPs aged 16 and above with an IEP that includes appropriate measurable postsecondary goals that are annually updated and based upon an age appropriate transition assessment, transition services, including courses of study, that will reasonably enable the student to meet those postsecondary goals, and annual IEP goals related to the student's transition services needs. There also must be evidence that the student was invited to the IEP Team meeting where transition services are to be discussed and evidence that, if appropriate, a representative of any participating agency was invited to the IEP Team meeting with the prior consent of the parent or student who has reached the age of majority. (20 U.S.C. § 1416[a][3][B])

The transition planning process is incorporated into the transition IEP. Figure 2.1 shows the required components to help guide the student's transition IEP and to identify services and activities needed to reach their postsecondary goals. Many state and local school districts use an Indicator 13 transition requirement checklist developed by the NSTTAC to ensure compliant transition IEPs (see www.nsttac.org).

Student-focused planning requires developing and teaching self-determination skills to ensure students are a part of the decisions that affect their postsecondary future. Starting in the early elementary years, planning activities should involve students in learning and practicing self-determination skills and continue throughout their educational career and adult years (Palmer, 2010). At the secondary level, this requires that the student work with a variety of individuals representing education (internal supports) and adult agencies (external supports) as described in the conceptual framework illustration in Chapter 1, to implement his or her transition IEP. The student must learn and apply self-advocacy skills, understand their strengths, interests, and preferences to advocate for him or herself. Therefore, recommended practice is to go beyond the law and not only invite the student to the meeting where the transition IEP is going to be discussed, but also ensure the student is actively involved and participating in the process by practicing and demonstrating his or her self-determination skills.

The NSTTAC (www.nsttac.org) is funded by the U.S. Department of Education, OSEP. NSTTAC work centers around the following objectives:

- Assist state education agencies with collecting data on IDEA (2004) Part B SPP Indicator 13 and using these data to improve transition services

- Generate knowledge that provides a foundation for states to improve transition services that enhance postschool outcomes

- Build capacity of states and local educational agencies to implement effective transition education and services that improve postschool outcomes

- Disseminate information to state personnel, practitioners, researchers, parents, and students regarding effective transition education and services that improve postschool outcomes.

(From National Secondary Transition Technical Assistance Center. [2013]. *NSTTAC objectives*. Charlotte, NC: Author. Retrieved from http://www.nsttac.org/)

The ongoing transition process builds upon skills, activities, and experiences over the years. Students (and families) continue to learn about themselves, refine and define their postsecondary goals, and leave school with a picture of their strengths, preferences, interests, and needs in order to move successfully to the postsecondary environments. A student's strengths, preferences, interests, and needs become the guidepost in developing annual goals and transition services throughout the educational years.

Starting in the early elementary years, planning activities should involve students in learning and practicing self-determination skills and continue throughout their educational career and adult years (Palmer, 2010).

Sitlington and Clark (2006, pp. 120–122) developed four key questions to help guide the transition planning process.

1. What do I already know about this student that would be helpful in developing postsecondary outcomes?

2. What information do I need to know about this individual to determine postsecondary goals?

3. What methods (e.g., transition assessments, activities, or experiences) will provide the information?

4. How will the assessment data be collected and used in the IEP process?

Following the components outlined in Figure 2.1, the remainder of this section will explain each of the required components of the transition IEP using the four questions as guides.

Present Levels of Performance

Question 1 relates to what we already know about this student that is depicted in the first area of Figure 2.1, the transition IEP process and the required components. The first area starts with the present level of academic and functional performance of the student, including age-appropriate transition assessment that is based on the student's strengths, preferences, interests, and needs.

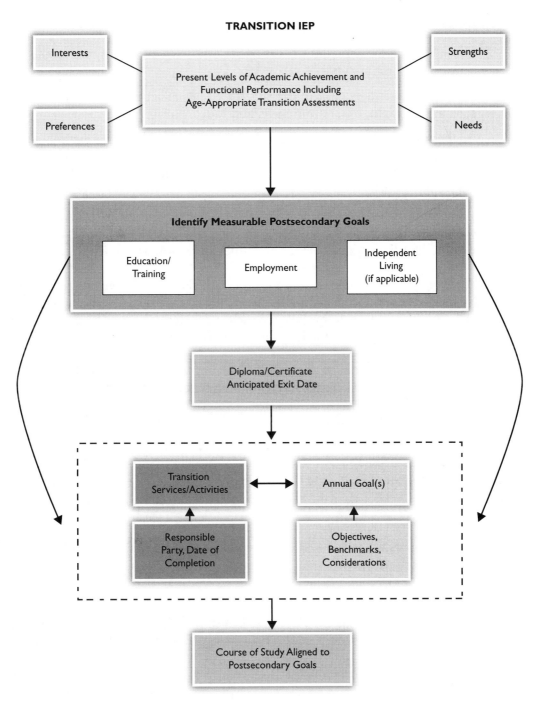

Figure 2.1. The transition IEP planning process. (Adapted by permission from Indiana Department of Education [2007]. *Transition IEP*.)

Referencing the skills acquired by achieving the previous years' goals, the student's academic and behavioral performance are addressed, as they relates to grade- or age-level performance, as defined by state standards or other curriculum. The statement of the student's present level of performance must

- Be relevant and connected to the student's disability and needs

- Show how the disability affects his or her involvement or progress in the general education curriculum

- Be functional and evident in the student's routine activities of daily living in settings such as classroom, bus, community, and lunchroom

- Be the starting point from which this year's progress is to be measured and evaluated. It becomes the baseline data to the proposed annual goals (and short-term objectives or benchmarks) to be included in the IEP using the same procedures and criteria of measurement (McGrath, 2009)

The present levels of academic and functional performance also include the age-appropriate transition assessment. The Division of Career Development and Transition of the Council for Exceptional Children defines transition assessment as the

> Ongoing process of collecting data on the individual's needs, preferences, and interests as they related to the demands of current and future working, educational, living and personal and social environments. Assessment data form the basis for defining goals and services to be included in the IEP. (Sitlington, Neubert, & Leconte, 1997, pp. 70–71)

Summarizing the findings of the transition assessments helps to highlight and distinguish between the student's strengths, interests, preferences, and needs, as described as follows:

- Strengths: Skills and attributes that the student is good at and helps describe other characteristics (physical /mental)

- Interests: Something that draws attention and curiosity and engages a student

- Preferences: Students' liking or disliking of an object, experience, situation, or setting

- Needs: Accommodations or supports needed to participate and perform at the established standard or criteria

So let's look at Myisha and Brad as we summarize their present levels of academic and functional performance including transition assessment.

 ## Myisha's Present Levels of Academic and Functional Performance, Including Transition Assessments

Myisha is a 17-year old student with a specific learning disability in reading fluency, reading comprehension, written expression, and oral language processing. According to her parents, she likes school. Around her friends and family, Myisha is outgoing and witty. She plays soccer on the junior varsity team at her high school. She hopes to make the varsity team this year. She has plans with a group of friends on most weekend evenings. This summer, she plans to get a part-time job.

Myisha demonstrates strengths related to managing money but struggles with use of calendars or other planners. In reading, teacher records indicate that Myisha reads at an eighth-grade level with fluency but struggles with oral reading comprehension and written expression at the fourth-grade level. Myisha's reading and writing performance require accommodations for testing and participation in the general curriculum, including extended time, read-aloud, and computer software resources to support listening comprehension and writing.

Myisha becomes anxious in new situations or around people she does not know. Recently, she told her mother that she is embarrassed by her disability. Her mother shared that these feelings deter Myisha from discussing her disability with her teachers and asking them for additional help or from telling her friends about her disability status. During her freshman year, she chose not to attend her IEP meeting, even though her teachers and parents encouraged her to attend. Last year, she attended the IEP meeting but participated passively by signing forms, making few comments throughout the meeting, and making little eye contact with the other team members present.

Myisha has maintained a 2.3 GPA for the past 2 years and is working toward a regular high school diploma. Her teachers say she does well when she is interested in the topic; however, at times she draws in class. This causes her to miss information that she then must make up at home by reading the textbook, which can be an arduous task given her problems with reading comprehension. Her English teacher stated that she would really benefit from a strategy that prompts her to pay attention for the whole class session so she can review her notes in the evening, rather than playing catch-up to gain missed information. Currently, Myisha receives special education services in an inclusive setting as well as in a resource setting. She also attends a weekly study skills session with a special education teacher who works on the development of independent study and organizational skills. She has passed the math portion of the state proficiency test but will retake the English portion.

Myisha recently got her driver's license. The independent living skills assessment shows she is capable of living on her own with support from her family. Based on her learning style assessment, Myisha is a visual learner. Her self-determination assessment shows she continues to need help with decision making, organizational skills, understanding her accommodation needs, and advocating for herself. She continues to be interested in going to college and studying in the health care field, including nursing.

 ## Brad's Present Levels of Academic and Functional Performance, Including Transition Assessments

Brad is 17 years old and has been diagnosed with autism spectrum disorder and attention-deficit/hyperactivity disorder (ADHD). He can carry on adult conversations and is well liked by his teachers. He has benefited from peer support and seems to do fine with transitions to different environments or tasks. He is a visual learner and benefits from visual supports throughout his day. He is good at noticing small details and likes hands-on activities.

All of Brad's core academic classes are in a special-education, self-contained setting and taught by a special education teacher who is highly qualified. Brad's science teacher indicated that Brad does quite well in class. He seems to thrive with hands-on activities. He also benefits from structured classes. Brad is getting mostly Bs, Cs, and Ds in classes, with an overall GPA of 2.0, and is working on a regular high school diploma. He works hard in all his classes and completes his assignments to the best of his ability. He is performing at the seventh- to eighth-grade level for reading and math but has difficulty with reading comprehension, math, and handwriting. He completes his work at school but does not always turn in his homework. He struggles with attention, organizational, and study skills. He will complete the state proficiency test again for English and algebra.

Brad's parents are supportive and are actively involved in his education. They state that it is difficult to get him up and ready for school in the morning. He wishes school would start later because he has a hard time with mornings. Many days he has trouble with his peers, especially those students who do not follow "the rules," who yell, or who make the classroom too noisy for him. His parents shared their concern that Brad does not have a peer group to socialize with on weekends.

He currently takes Adderall. He has benefited from a peer mentor and some social skills training. His peers know when he is getting frustrated by his body language. He could benefit from strategies to help him cope when he is frustrated and anxious.

Brad continues to have a strong interest in working on cars and one day wants to open up his own auto repair shop. He will start at the Career-Tech Center in auto mechanics next semester. Based on Brad's career interest inventory and other prior assessments, he loves taking things apart and putting them back together. He also needs an environment where he can move around. His self-determination assessment showed his need to understand his disability and accommodation needs, including coping strategies when frustrated. The IEP team does have a concern about Brad's ability to handle the noise level in an auto mechanic shop setting.

Brad is working on getting his driver's license this year with the help of his parents. He and his parents anticipate that Brad will remain living with them for at least the next several years. They do want to support him living in his own place one day.

The first question as described by Sitlington and Clark (2006) in transition planning process is meant to provide a basic overall profile of a student's strengths, preferences, interests, and needs. The second question is to determine what additional information you need to know to help the student develop his or her postsecondary goals and continue to develop the student profile. By exploring the answers to this question with the students, you will capture meaningful and important details that help guide the next steps of the process. The profile should become clearer and more defined as the student gets closer to graduating from high school, with each year asking, "What else do I need to know about this student in helping them develop and meet their postsecondary goals?"

For middle school students, answers to the questions tend to be broader. For example, many middle school students have big dreams, such as being a National Football League (NFL) player or a rock star, that may or may not match their current activities or skill sets. For the student who wants to be an NFL player, the first piece of information is to determine what activities he is currently engaged in, such as playing on a football team and academic skills. The job of teachers is to present the data and help students make informed choices, rather than squelching dreams. In addition, since the student has a strong interest in football, greater in-depth inquiry may be needed to understand his interests and help him research other careers related to football, sports, or alternative options.

The third question is related to the transition methods that will provide the information for Brad and Myisha. The methods and information gained will be built upon over the years from middle school through graduation. The methods could be transition assessments, transition services and activities (e.g., job shadowing), or specific courses or programs the student may complete to gain the necessary skills and knowledge that relate to their postsecondary goals (e.g., auto mechanics program for Brad). Assessments about a student's strengths, preferences, interests, and needs must be "matched" to expectations and demands of the postsecondary environments of education/training, employment, and independent living, as illustrated in Figure 2.2 (Sitlington, Neubert, Begun, Lombard, & LeConte, 2007). For example, a number of transition activities could occur to help a middle school student move toward refining his goal of playing professional football such as researching requirements to get into the NFL (e.g., obtaining high school diploma, possibly attending college, playing on high school and college football teams, interviewing people, etc.). A thorough student assessment using age-appropriate methods listed in the box on the left of Figure 2.2 should occur. Next, an assessment of the potential environments (NFL player) should be carried out using the methods in the box on the right of Figure 2.2. A comparison will then help determine if there is a match between the student and the environment(s) of the desired career. The "Is There a Match?" box identifies next steps, depending on whether or not there is a match.

Finally and most importantly as stated in question four, data must not only be collected but used in the transition IEP process for driving instruction and services to help students reach their postsecondary goals. Table 2.1 provides examples of information that

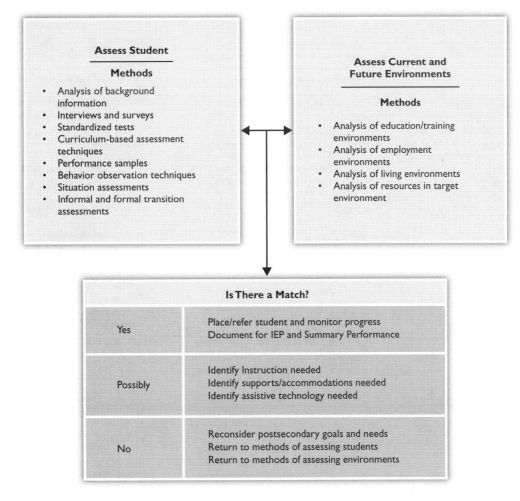

Figure 2.2. Transition assessment: Matching for success. (From *Assess to success: a practitioner's handbook on transition assessment* by Sitlington, Patricia L. Copyright 2007 Reproduced with permission of SAGE PUBLICATIONS INC BOOKS in the format Republish in a textbook and "other" book via Copyright Clearance Center.)

Table 2.1.   Guiding questions for transition planning

Question[a]	Myisha	Brad
1. What do I already know about this student that would be helpful in developing postsecondary outcomes?	• Is a visual learner • Participates in extracurricular activities • Supportive parents • Struggles with reading comprehension and written expression • Needs to pass English portion of the state proficiency test • Is embarrassed by her disability • GPA of 2.3 • Has driver's license • Good at managing money • Transition assessments have been conducted that identified her self-determination skill needs. • Becomes anxious in new situations	• Is a visual learner • Supportive parents • High interest in cars and getting his driver's license • Struggles with reading comprehension, math and handwriting • Needs to pass the state proficiency test • Needs organizational and study skills • GPA of 2.0 • Has difficulty socializing with peers • Needs coping strategies when frustrated • Transition assessments have been conducted that identified his self-determination skill needs. • Needs an environment where he can move around
2. What information do I need to know about this individual to determine postsecondary goals?	• What other health care careers might Myisha be interested in? • What specific learning strategies help her for reading comprehension? • What does she understand about her disability? • What postsecondary options are available in Myisha's community or state that will meet her needs?	• Since Brad does well in science and hands-on activities, what other career opportunities may be available for him in addition to auto mechanics? • Brad expressed a desire to open up his own repair shop. What classes and activities have helped him explore the feasibility of this option? • Due to Brad's autism and the environment of the auto mechanics industry, could Brad's sensitivity to odors, lighting, or other environmental factors be a challenge?
3. What methods (e.g., transition assessments, activities or experiences) will provide the information?	• Teachers can find out what the guidance counselors are using with all other students such as O*Net, an online resource for career exploration and job analysis with detailed–descriptions of various occupations (http://www .onetonline.org/). • Teachers can utilize a curriculum such as 411 Disclosure or another online curriculum such as the Youthhood, for Myisha to help her understand her disability and learn self-determination skills such as decision-making, problem-solving, and self-advocacy skills. • Myisha can meet with the guidance counselor to explore college options for her field of study (e.g., health care) and job shadow in a health care setting. • Myisha can attend college night at the high school and gather information about the various colleges and degrees.	• Teachers can find out what guidance counselors do with all other students including Career-Tech assessments such as O*Net (see Myisha's column). • Teachers can work with Brad on assessing his self-determination and self-advocacy skills as well as understanding his support needs when frustrated. • Teachers can use online curriculum such as Youthhood (see Myisha's column) or JobTIPS, which looks at environmental demands. • Brad can participate in a job shadow with an auto mechanic or enroll in the business foundations class. • Brad can attend Career-Tech center for auto mechanics.
4. How will the assessment data be collected and used in the IEP process?	• Myisha will identify other health care professions and the educational requirements needed with support from the guidance counselor. • Myisha will complete the lessons in Youthhood to understand her disability and will discuss with her resource teacher. • Myisha and her parents will attend college night at the high school.	• Brad and his parents will complete the Planning for Community Life assessment and results will be included in the IEP. • Brad will work with the guidance counselor using O*Net to explore other occupations related to auto mechanics to give Brad more options. • Brad will begin to explore JobTIPS web site with support from his resource teacher. • Information from his Career-Tech program will be included in the IEP.

[a]*Source:* Sitlington and Clark (2006).

could be gathered using these questions to guide the planning process for Myisha and Brad along with the online resource examples. Additional resources can be found in the list at the end of this chapter.

Measurable Postsecondary Goals

With the information for Myisha and Brad, the next step in developing the transition IEP is identifying measurable postsecondary goals (see second section of the Figure 2.1 flowchart). A postsecondary goal is one that a child hopes to achieve after leaving high school (NSTTAC, 2011). As stated in Table 2.2, IDEA (2004) requires a measurable postsecondary goal in the areas of education/training, employment, and when necessary, independent living. The measurable postsecondary goal statement articulates what the student would like to achieve after high school; is based on the student's strengths, preferences, and interests, as well as on age-appropriate transition assessment; and can be measured. Definitions for each of the areas include

Education—2- or 4-year college or university, technical college; *or*

Training—specific vocational or career field training, independent living skill training, vocational training program, apprenticeship, on-the-job-training (OJT), job corps, etc.

Employment—paid competitive employment (including supported), and military

If needed, Independent Living Skills—daily living skills, independent living, residential supports, financial, transportation, community resources, mobility orientation, using interpreter services, etc. (NSTTAC; www.nsttac.org)

Throughout the student's transition years, information gathered will help refine or redefine their postsecondary goals. For example, a student in middle school or early high school may want to become a doctor, even though he does not have a strong background in the sciences. As information is gathered through coursework, course projects, transition assessments, activities, and other experiences, his postsecondary goal for employment will become more aligned with his strengths, interests, preferences, and needs. He may refine his goal to obtain a career in the health field such as an x-ray technician, physician's assistant, or a different career. Now, look at Myisha and Brad's goals.

Table 2.2.   Student-focused planning: From legislation to practice

Category	IDEA (2004) legislation [34 CFR 300.320(b)] [20 U.S.C.1414(d)(1)(B)]	Practice
Student-focused planning	• Beginning no later than the first IEP to be in effect when the child is 16 years of age (14 in many states) and updated annually thereafter where transition is to be discussed, students must be invited to attend the transition IEP meeting. • IEP must include a statement of appropriate measurable postsecondary goals based upon age-appropriate transition assessments related to training, education, employment and, where appropriate, independent living skills. • A statement of measurable annual goals, including academic and functional goals designed to support and aligns with the student's postsecondary goals. • The transition services, including course of study needed to assist the child to reach those goals.	• Student involvement in the planning process • Self-determination skills training • Self-advocacy skill training • Person-centered planning strategies • Using assessments (informal and formal assessments) to inform the planning process

Key: IEP, individualized education program.

 ## Myisha's Postsecondary Goals

Education/Training: Myisha will enroll in a two-year nursing program at the community college.
Employment: Myisha will obtain a job as a nurse after completing her nursing program.
Independent living: Based on the independent living skills assessment and interview with Myisha and her parents, she has a driver's license, manages money, demonstrates age-appropriate life skills, and participates in extracurricular activities. Additional support will be provided by her parents; therefore Myisha does not need an independent living goal.

 ## Brad's Postsecondary Goals

Education/Training: Brad will receive on-the-job-training in the auto mechanics field from the employer.
Employment: Brad will obtain a job as an auto mechanic or related position.
Independent living: Based on the independent living skills assessment and interview with Brad and his parents, he is working toward getting his driver's license and plans to continue to live with his parents for the next several years. He demonstrates appropriate life, money, safety, and social skills. Brad and his parents feel that the parents will provide the support he will need and do not see a need for an independent living goal.

Diploma-Certificate Decision

The third section of the transition IEP flowchart is the discussion of diploma and/or certificate. For many "high stakes" testing states, in order to obtain the state diploma, the student must past the state proficiency test or the end-of-course assessments. In a national study of graduation requirements and diploma options, Johnson, Thurlow, and Stout (2007) found that 24 states required youth with and without disabilities to pass an exit exam to receive a high school diploma. Based on the information from the Present Levels section with supporting data, difficult conversations about preparing for such exams or understanding the implications of alternative pathways must occur with the student and family early in their high school experience (freshman and sophomore years) to ensure appropriate educational programming can be developed to meet their postschool outcomes. For Myisha and Brad, both are working toward a regular high school diploma.

Annual Goals and Transition Services

The next two areas are side-by-side on the flowchart (Figure 2.1) because they are driven by the present levels of performance and transition service needs. A statement of measurable annual goals for the transition IEP, including academic and functional goals are designed to support and align with the student's postsecondary goals. So for Myisha and Brad, we would begin by asking

- What are the measurable goals that are aligned to the general education curriculum and address the needs of Myisha (e.g., reading comprehension, reading fluency, written expression) and Brad (e.g., reading comprehension, math, organizational skills, study skills)?

- How and what type of instruction will occur to help the student learn what he or she needs to learn this year (e.g., direct instruction, teaching learning strategies, reading, math, organizational skills, study skills, self-determination skills)?

- What other typical transition services can the student access that are currently available within the high school (e.g., working with guidance counselor, attending a Career-Tech program, attending college night for information, etc.)?

- What other transition services and community experiences will be provided (e.g., job shadowing for Myisha and Brad)? (NSTTAC, 2007)

Course of Study

The final section of the transition IEP flowchart is the course of study. The course of study is a multiyear description of coursework to achieve the student's desired postschool goals, from the student's current to anticipated exit year. There are many electives offered in high schools that can assist students in acquiring the essential life skills needed for future environments (e.g., study skills, career planning, interpersonal relationships, adult roles and responsibilities, personal finance, child development and parenting).

Student Development

The foundation for student development is the range of experiences and skill development that prepare students for adult roles and responsibilities after high school. Having access to quality instruction and the general education curriculum is important for effective student development and requires that accommodations and supports be available and planned for so that the student may be successful in school and community environments. Student development activities include academic instruction, work-based learning, extracurricular activities, career and vocational curriculum, assessment, and life skill instruction based on the needs of the student (Kohler, 1998).

Quality instruction is the foundation of good transition practices and outcomes. Chapter 3 will highlight quality academic instruction, and Chapter 4 will bring instruction and transition together. Areas such as UDL, differentiated instruction, appropriate learning strategies, and much more will be covered. Work-based learning and career development is taught through career-tech programs and community settings as well as specific classes. Life skills (e.g., personal finance, nutrition and wellness, government, adult roles and responsibilities, career orientation) can be taught in a variety of classes as well as directly taught in classrooms, school, or community settings. See the resource list at the end of the chapter for information on evidence-based practices, lesson starters, and curriculum materials.

A variety of work-based learning experiences are identified, starting with in-school jobs and building upon the skills to allow students to have experiences through job shadowing, paid and nonpaid work experiences, internships, and service learning. Table 2.3 shows what is required by law and examples of practices to fulfill the legal requirements.

Family Involvement

Parent and family involvement has been shown to improve academic outcomes for all students. A large body of research has shown the positive benefits of parent–professional collaboration on the education of students with disabilities (Henderson & Mapp, 2002). In the context of transition education, family involvement includes participation, empowerment,

Table 2.3. Student development: From legislation to practice

Category	IDEA 2004 legislation [§602 (34) (A)]	Practice
Student development	• The coordinated set of activities must be based on the individual child's needs taking into account the child's strengths, preferences, and interests, and includes instruction, related services, community experiences, the development of employment and other postschool objectives, and, when appropriate, acquisition of daily living skills and functional vocational evaluation.	• Academic instruction that utilizes differentiated instruction and UDL • Teaching learning strategies • Identification and development of adaptations and accommodations • Academic and behavior assessments • Social skill training • Self-determination skills training • Life-skill instruction • Career-Tech curriculum • Work-related skills and behaviors • Career assessments and exploration • Work-study programs • Job shadowing • Apprenticeships • Internships • Structured work experiences • Mentorships • Service learning • Paid work

and training (see Table 2.4). Family involvement strategies should encourage families to become involved in planning and delivering transition-focused education and services at the student, school, and community levels.

To be effective, families must be engaged in a meaningful way and have opportunities for training to ensure a strong partnership with educators and service providers. Attitude, socioeconomic status, culture, communication skills, and fears can be barriers or obstacles to effective family involvement and partnerships with schools (Geneen, Powers, & Lopez-Vasquez, 2006). According to Henderson (2007; as cited in Fostering parent and professional collaboration research brief, PACER Center, pp. 8), in order for parents to be a true partner with professionals, several conditions must be present.

To be effective, families must be engaged in a meaningful way and have opportunities for training to ensure a strong partnership with educators and service providers. Attitude, socioeconomic status, culture, communication skills, and fears can be barriers or obstacles to effective family involvement and partnerships with schools (Geneen, Powers, & Lopez-Vasquez, 2006).

1. Families need to feel welcome in their child's school. They must feel they are appreciated for whatever level or type of parental involvement they are able to provide.

2. Families need to feel a connection with the staff, school and other parents/families.

3. Some parents may not become engaged until they receive specific invitations with clear instructions on how to be involved in school. In addition, they may need specific and clear instructions on how to assist their child's learning at home.

For parents and families of transition-age youth, the partnership with schools become even more critical when considering the various postschool environments their child must be prepared to enter.

Table 2.4. Family involvement: From Legislation to Practice

Category	IDEA 2004 legislation [§614(A)(VII)(cc)]	Practice
Family Involvement	• Written notice, parent consent, procedural safeguards, and all other parent rights as defined by IDEA for implementing special education provisions • Beginning no later than one year before the student becomes 18 years of age, a statement that the student and the parent have been informed that parent's rights … will transfer to the student at 18 years of age.	• School personnel can help parents identify strengths, preferences, interests and needs in their child. • School personnel can encourage choice making. • School personnel can demonstrate problem-solving skills. • School personnel can follow-through on commitments and communication. • School personnel can ensure information is disseminated in the preferred style of the family. • Parents can serve as mentors and trainers. • Families can attend and participate at IEP meetings. • Information can be disseminated in a family-friendly format and in time to effectively plan. • Support networks for families can be encouraged. • Families can receive training on topics such as transition IEP planning process, legal issues, advocacy skill development, and agencies and services. • Families can participate on decision-making committees. • Families can participate in policy development and program evaluation.

Key: IEP, individualized education program.

Interagency Collaboration

Interagency collaboration refers to schools, community agencies, organizations, higher education, and businesses working together collectively to promote a seamless system of transition for positive postschool outcomes. Interagency collaboration in the unified framework illustration in Chapter 1 (Figure 1.1) is considered external supports. As students leave school, they leave a system of entitlement (e.g. free and appropriate public education) and move to an adult service-delivery system based on eligibility requirements for supports. Therefore, it is imperative that local and statewide organizations and agencies understand each other's roles and responsibilities, are clear as to how they can work together to benefit the student, and plan in a way to avoid gaps and/or duplication of services (see Table 2.5). Agencies

Table 2.5. Interagency collaboration: From legislation to practice

Category	IDEA 2004 legislation [§614(5)(B)(ii)]	Practice
Interagency collaboration	• School personnel must provide to the parent and student written information on various state and local adult agencies to facilitate the movement from high school to adult life. • School personnel must invite adult agencies who will be responsible for providing or paying for any transition services. • Schools must provide a summary of academic and functional performance, including recommendations to assist the student in meeting postsecondary goals, for students whose eligibility terminates because of graduation with a regular high school diploma or because of exceeding the age eligibility for under state law	• Coordinated and shared delivery of transition related services with service providers • Collaborative use and development of assessment data including Summary of Performance • Coordinated sharing of service information to student and families • Collaboration between higher education institutions and the school district • Procedures for sharing student information are established and followed • Interagency or community transition team include all key stakeholders and make data-based decisions • Methods of communication among service providers are established • Roles of service providers are clearly articulated • Identification and reduction of system barriers to collaboration through local transition councils • State level teams conduct regular policy analysis to identify gaps and conflicts

such as Vocational Rehabilitation Services, Mental Health and Developmental Disabilities, Workforce Development, colleges and universities, local community rehabilitation agencies or employment service providers, Social Security Administration, transportation, housing, juvenile justice, and others are key players to a seamless transition service delivery.

IDEA 2004 requires students to have a summary of performance (SOP) as they graduate high school or exit due to exceeding the eligible age of the state. The SOP must summarize the student's academic and functional performance, including recommendations to assist the student in meeting postsecondary goals. Most states or local districts have their own SOP form and these are given to students at the end of their high school years. Ideally, the SOP becomes a tool for students to use to apply their self-determination and self-advocacy skills by sharing the document with adult agencies to aid in eligibility of services and program development. See a sample of the SOP at the end of the chapter.

Program Structures

Program structures are features that relate to efficient and effective delivery of transition-focused education and services. These features include program philosophy, planning, policy, evaluation, and resource development (see Table 2.6). Practices that promote positive transition outcomes are strategic planning, attention to cultural competency, clearly articulated mission and values, qualified staff members, and sufficient allocation of resources (Kohler, 1998). For example, all students take part in career counseling activities with the guidance counselor or participate in an internship part of their senior project. Program structures can enhance transition outcomes when resources are shared and meet the needs of all students, as described in Chapter 1 and will be further explained in Chapters 3 and 4.

SUMMARY

This chapter provides a brief overview of quality transition practices, from the early stages of planning through postsecondary options. It summarized the legal requirements for transition services, the transition component requirements of an IEP and how to develop

Table 2.6. Program structures: From legislation to practice

Category	IDEA (2004) legislation [§300.114]	Practice
Program structures	• Least-restrictive environment (LRE) means that a student with a disability should have the opportunity to be educated with their nondisabled peers to the greatest extent appropriate. They should have access to the general education curriculum, extracurricular activities, and other programs and activities that other nondisabled peers have access to. The student should be provided with supplementary aids and services necessary to achieve educational goals in settings with their nondisabled peers.	• Students are educated alongside their nondisabled peers. • Students have opportunities to participate in extracurricular activities. • Educators share responsibility and accountability for all students. • Work-based learning occurs in integrated settings. • Culturally responsive practices are applied at all levels of the organization. • Student transitions are planned for across all educational levels. • Decisions are data based. • Program evaluations are ongoing and used for improvement. • Policies support the mission and values of the district. • Structures and processes are in place for systemic change.

a meaningful transition IEP, and practices to implement transition-focused education and services. The next chapter highlights effective instructional practices to ensure quality postsecondary outcomes.

FOR FURTHER INFORMATION

Additional Books in the Brookes Transition to Adulthood Series

Wehman, P. (2011). *Essentials of transition planning.* Baltimore, MD: Paul H. Brookes Publishing Co.

Overview of the transition planning process in general, with legal and practical considerations

Test, D. (2012). *Evidence-based instructional strategies for transition.* Baltimore, MD: Paul H. Brookes Publishing Co.

Methods for effectively teaching transition-related skills to youth with moderate and severe disabilities

Greene, G. (2011). *Transition planning for culturally and linguistically diverse youth.* Baltimore, MD: Paul H. Brookes Publishing Co.

Principles and strategies for sensitively working with students and families from culturally and linguistically different backgrounds

Self-Determination

Benson, B.P., & Barnett, S.P. (2005). *Student-led conferencing: Using showcase portfolios.* Thousand Oaks, CA: Corwin Press.

Strategies for students to gather and present their work instead of traditional parent–teacher conferences

Thoma, C.A., & Wehman, P. (2010). *Getting the most out of IEPs: An educator's guide to the student-directed approach.* Baltimore, MD: Paul H. Brookes Publishing Co.

Shows how students can be more involved in and even lead their IEP, increasing motivation and self-advocacy skills

Wehmeyer, M.L., & Field, S.L. (2007). *Self-determination: Instructional and assessment strategies.* Thousand Oaks, CA: Corwin Press.

Practical guidance on empowering students to make their own decisions

Wehmeyer, M.L., & Palmer, S.B. (2012). *Whose future is it?* [Instructor's guide, Student reader and Workbook]. Verona, WI: Attainment Company, Inc.

A curriculum that fosters self-determination skills by guiding the student through planning for adulthood

Online Transition Assessment Resources

Iowa Transition Assessment

This web site (http://transitionassessment.northcentralrrc.org/) provides resources and tools to assist in developing a transition IEP in order to identify a student's interests, preferences, strengths and needs in order for the student to meet their postschool goals.

JobTIPS

This online program (http://www.do2learn.com/JobTIPS/index.html) is designed to help young adults and adults with disabilities, such as autism spectrum disorder and other disabilities, to explore career interests and be successful in their jobs. This web site also looks at the environmental demands, including social and behavioral challenges that may have an impact an individual seeking and obtaining employment.

Skills to Pay the Bills: Mastering Soft Skills for Workplace Success

Designed to introduce youth to workplace interpersonal and professional skills, this curriculum (http://www.dol.gov/odep/topics/youth/softskills/) is targeted to youth ages 14 to 21 in both in- and out-of-school environments. The program comprises hands-on, engaging activities that focus on six key skill areas: communication, enthusiasm and attitude, teamwork, networking, problem solving and critical thinking, and professionalism.

The 411 on Disability Disclosure: A Workbook for Youth with Disabilities

Teaching young adults how and when to disclose their disability is an important skill. Developed for youth to learn about disability disclosure, this downloadable workbook (http://www.ncwd-youth.info/411-on-disability-disclosure) helps young people make informed decisions about whether or not to disclose their disability and understand how that decision may have an impact on their education, employment, and social lives.

The Youthhood

This is an interactive curriculum-based tool (http://www.youthhood.org) that can help young adults plan for life after high school. Although the site addresses youth directly, it is intended to be used as a curriculum within a classroom, community program, or in any setting where adults are working with youth to set goals and plan for the future.

Evidence-Based Lesson Planning

National Secondary Transition Technical Assistance Center

Go to www.nsttac.org and select *Evidence Based Practices* in the field of secondary transition to view studies under each of the taxonomy categories as well as *Lesson Plan Library* to support each of the categories.

Zarrow Center for Learning Enrichment at the University of Oklahoma

The web site (http://www.ou.edu/content/education/centers-and-partnerships/zarrow .html?rd=1) offers two sets of useful transition education materials (select the Transition Education Materials button on the sidebar). First, *ME! Lessons for Teaching Self-Awareness and Self-Advocacy* are used to help and teach students about their disability and abilities, rights and responsibilities, and self-advocacy skills. During the lessons students develop a portfolio containing information and to help themselves transition from high school to postschool settings. Second, the *Student-Directed Transition Planning (SDTP) Lesson Materials* teaches students to complete their self-directed SOP. With input from families and educators, students determine their postschool goals and learn various aspects about themselves. SDTP offers a detailed teacher's guide with step-by-step instructional suggestions. Tools include PowerPoint presentations and pencil and paper activities.

iTransition: It's All About Me!

iTransition (http://www.pepnet.org/itransition) is a free, online transition curriculum to help students with a hearing impairments prepare for the future. Four separate trainings with activities help students learn about themselves, their career goals, and the skills they need to be successful in after high school.

Appendix A

Summary of My Performance

Section I: My Background Information		
Name:		**Date:**
Date of birth:	**Year of graduation/exit:**	**e-mail:**
Street address:		
City/state/zip:		
Home telephone:		**Cell phone:**
Primary disability:		**Secondary disability, if applicable:**

Section II: My Perception of My Disability	
Strengths:	
Interests/preferences:	
Challenges:	
My disability impact on learning and/or mobility:	

Supports and accommodations what works:	**Setting** ___ Distraction free ___ Adaptive furniture ___ Special lighting ___ Other:
	Timing/Scheduling ___ Extra time to complete assignments ___ Frequent breaks ___ Flexible schedule ___Other:
	Response ___Assistive technology ___ Braille ___ Colored overlays ___ Dictate words to scribe
	___ Word processor/computer ___ Taped responses ___ Other:
	Presentation ___ Large print ___ Braille ___Assistive devices ___ Magnifier ___ Read or sign items ___ Use of calculator ___ Shortened instructions ___ Reread directions ___Visual schedule ___ Use of assignment/notebook/organizer ___ Other:
What does not work:	

Adapted by permission from Indiana Department of Education (2007). *Summary of My Performance.*
In *Teaching Transition Skills in Inclusive Schools* by Teresa Grossi, Ph.D., and Cassandra M. Cole, Ed.D.
(2013, Paul H. Brookes Publishing Co., Inc.)

 (continued)

Summary of My Performance *(continued)*

Section III: My Postschool Goals	
Living	My goal:
	Accommodations and/or supports, including adult agencies that may help in achieving goal:
Learning	My goal:
	Accommodations and/or supports, including adult agencies that may help in achieving goal:
Working	My goal:
	Accommodations and/or supports, including adult agencies that may help in achieving goal:

Section IV: My Summary of Present Level of Academic Achievement and Functional Performance
(Consider transcripts, attach IEP, and other appropriate assessments.)

I have accomplished the following academic achievements:

I have accomplished the following in the area of functional achievements:

There are numerous assessment reports that help identify my achievements and support the documentation of my disability and assist in planning for my postschool education or work. Please attach the most recent WAIS, Woodcock-Johnson (if conducted) or appropriate assessments.

__ Psychological/cognitive	__ Response to intervention (RTI)	__ Reading assessments
__ Neuropsychological	__ Language proficiency assessments	__ Medical/physical
__ Achievement/academics	__ Communication	__ Adaptive behavior __ Behavioral analysis
__ Social/interpersonal skills	__ Assistive technology	__ Self-determination
__ Community-based assessment	__ Career/vocational/transition assessments	__ Other:

Section V: Important People or Agencies Who May Help Me Achieve My Postschool Goals

__ Vocational rehabilitation services (phone number) : _____

__ College/university support services (phone number): _____

__ Bureau of Developmental Disabilities: (phone number) : _____

__ Adult agency provider (name/number): _____

__ Other: _____

Student signature: _____   Teacher of record signature: _____

Adapted by permission from Indiana Department of Education (2007). *Summary of My Performance.*
In *Teaching Transition Skills in Inclusive Schools* by Teresa Grossi, Ph.D., and Cassandra M. Cole, Ed.D.
(2013, Paul H. Brookes Publishing Co., Inc.)

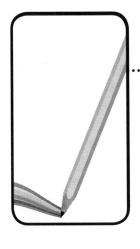

3

A Solid Instructional Foundation for Positive Postschool Outcomes

The foundation for positive postschool outcomes, as shown in the conceptual framework in Chapter 1, begins with access to quality instruction, academic rigor and standards, personalization, career exploration, and inclusive practices. This foundation should begin in the early elementary years and continue through graduation. We will look at each of these essential components in this chapter.

It cannot be emphasized enough that *how* students experience school, academically, socially, and emotionally, will determine postschool life. While having access to quality transition services is important, it isn't enough. Students must have access to the general education standards and high quality instruction in inclusive environments. They must feel a sense of "belonging" to their school and have a system of support in place for social and emotional development. Often, transition services are seen as something separate from the other experiences that students have in school. In fact, quality transition services are *dependent* on the kind of access students have to rigor, standards, and high quality instruction.

KEY CONCEPTS FOR QUALITY INSTRUCTION

There is a growing body of research to indicate that schools make a difference in student achievement, and a substantial portion of that difference can be attributed to teachers. The quality of teaching is the most important factor that influences student learning. After an extensive review of research conducted in the 1970s, Brophy and Good (1986) refuted the myth that classroom teachers do not make a difference in student learning. In 1997, Wright, Horn and Sanders determined that the individual teacher can positively affect a wide range of students. They stated that "effective teachers appear to be effective with students of all achievement levels, regardless of the level of heterogeneity in their classrooms" (p. 67).

Studies reveal the impact schools and teachers can have on student achievement. A landmark study conducted by Sanders and Horn (1994, reviewed in Marzano, 2003) revealed a difference of 39 percentage points in achievement between students who had "most effective" teachers and students who had "least effective" teachers. In classrooms taught by teachers characterized as "most effective," students showed achievement gains of 53 percentage points over the course of one academic year. In contrast, in classrooms led by "least effective" teachers, student achievement gains averaged 14 percentage points.

31

Slavin (1995) draws on the early work by John Carroll (1963, 1989) to identify four critical elements of schools and classrooms that impact student learning. All four of these elements must be present for instruction to be effective. These elements are represented in Table 3.1.

Nine broad teaching strategies that have positive effects on student learning have been extracted from the research on effective instruction. Recommendations for implementing these nine research-based strategies are detailed in *Classroom Instruction That Works* (Dean, Hubbell, Pitler, & Stone (2012). These include

1. Identifying similarities and differences: Teaching students to identify similarities and differences allows them to understand content at a deeper level. Four ways that teachers can use this strategy are to a) explicitly present similarities and differences and directly point them out to students, b) ask students to independently identify similarities and differences, c) represent similarities and differences in graphic or symbolic format, and d) use comparing, classifying, metaphors, and analogies.

2. Summarizing and note taking: Summarizing information allows students to produce a condensed version of information that includes only important elements

Table 3.1.   Four elements of effective instruction

Element	Description	Examples
Quality of Instruction	The degree to which information or skills are presented so that students can easily learn them. This would include the quality of the curriculum (what we want students to know) and the quality of the lessons and activities that would help them learn.	• Present lessons in an organized fashion • Make transitions from one topic to another • Use images and examples • Restate key points • Relate lessons to students' background knowledge • Use advance organizers • Review and reteach • State lesson objectives clearly, showing the connection between what is taught and what is assessed • Provide frequent formal and informal assessment • Give immediate feedback
Appropriate levels of instruction	The degree the teacher knows the students' level of knowledge and skills and the degree to which the teacher ensures that the instruction is neither too difficult nor too easy for students	• Team-assisted individualization • Using strategies associated with differentiated instruction (see section on differentiated instruction) • Use preassessments to determine appropriate level for students • Offer multiple ways that students can access, understand, and apply learning • Use various means to understand the students: their readiness levels, their interests, and their learning preferences
Incentive	The degree to which the teacher ensures that students are motivated to learn the material being taught	• Relate topics to student's lives • Communicate high expectations to students • Reward students for academic and social growth • Increase a student's probability of success (zone of proximal development) • Ensure that students feel academically "safe" in the classroom by creating a community of learners grounded in respect and encouragement
Time	The degree to which students are given ample time to learn the material being taught	• Ensure that students are engaged during allocated time for instruction • Provide extended time to complete tasks when warranted

Source: Slavin (1995).

of the information. This provides an opportunity for students to concisely communicate what is important and serves as a way to check understanding. Notetaking is best when it is not verbatim and when the notes are subsequently used as a study guide.

3. Reinforcing effort and providing recognition: Not all students are aware that effort enhances achievement. Thus, teachers should explicitly explain and exemplify the "effort belief" to students. Recognition is more effective when it is abstract and symbolic rather than in the form of tangible rewards. Ensure that praise and recognition are provided for authentic standards of performance.

4. Homework and practice: Homework should always be a focused strategy to help students increase their understanding. While there is no clear answer on what the right amount of homework should be, students at the lower grades should be given less homework than secondary students. The level of difficulty should generally be such that students can work independently without relying on parental help. Educators should engage in conversations and discussions that help to clearly identify and articulate the purpose of homework (e.g., for practice and for preparation or elaboration), and this purpose should be shared by all staff and articulated to the school community. If homework is assigned, students should receive feedback on the homework.

5. Nonlinguistic representations: This refers to the imagery mode of representing information. Purposefully engaging students in the creation of nonlinguistic representations stimulates and increases brain activity. Examples include graphic organizers, physical models, creating mental pictures, drawing pictures, and physical movement.

6. Cooperative learning: When students are provided opportunities to work together and interact in a variety of ways, their learning is enhanced. There should be a variety of criteria to determine collaborative learning groups. Groups organized by ability should be used sparingly; groups should be kept small in size, and cooperative learning should be applied systematically and consistently but not overused.

7. Setting objectives and providing feedback: Goal setting provides direction for learning by helping students realize both the short and long-term expectations for learning. Goals should be flexible and specific. Feedback should provide students with an understanding of what they have learned and what they still need to learn, it should be timely, and it should connect to a specific knowledge or skill. Involving students in goal setting and feedback can increase student's accountability for their learning.

8. Generating and testing hypotheses: Inquiry in the classroom is important, as it allows students to deepen their understanding of key concepts. By asking students to generate and test a hypothesis, the teacher moves the student from a simple awareness of the information to a deeper understanding and application of the knowledge.

9. Cues, questions and advance organizers: This strategy helps students to connect what they already know to what they need to know. Giving cues, questions, and advanced organizers provides students with a "preview" of what they can expect with a lesson. Techniques related to this element of instruction help students retrieve what they have already learned and know about a topic.

How the Brain Learns

For many years, brain research and the technologies and science associated with this research were not something that was in the forefront of minds of many educators as they created their classroom environments. However, educators do not need a background in neuroscience to apply important concepts of brain research to their classrooms. One of the clearest and maybe most important

The important features of brain research provide a framework for teachers to understand their students' individual strengths, challenges, and preferences (Rose & Meyer, 2002).

understandings from the research on the brain is that our attempts to label or categorize students as "normal," "disabled," "slow," or "at risk" has caused us to miss important qualities of our students. The important features of brain research provide a framework for teachers to understand their students' individual strengths, challenges, and preferences (Rose & Meyer, 2002).

Research shows that the brain develops five learning systems: emotional , social, cognitive, physical, and reflective. All five systems work together in an interrelated fashion (Given, 2002).

1. Emotional learning system: It is important that teachers establish a learning environment that provides emotional safety and support to students. Emotions motivate students in both positive and negative ways and thus affect their ability to learn. Teachers who understand the link between emotion and learning can help students be more successful.

2. Social learning system: Socially, people desire to be respected, belong to a group, and enjoy attention from peers. The social system of learning focuses on the interpersonal experiences that we have with others. In schools, this requires that classrooms be communities where students are acknowledged for their strengths rather than focusing on their deficits.

3. Cognitive learning system: Attention to the cognitive learning system places teachers in the role of facilitator of learning, helping students connect new information to their existing knowledge. New information is best taught in thematic units in which new information is embedded, information is interrelated, and there is a connection to the real world of the student, rather than through rote memorization.

4. Physical learning system: This system involves learning that is active and engaging. Classrooms that engage the physical learning system provide opportunities for students to use manipulatives, construct their own learning materials, and be involved in hands-on activities.

5. Reflective learning system: When attending to this system, teachers guide students to understand their learning preferences and help them learn how to use them to develop their strengths. Additionally, the teacher helps students reflect on their weaknesses to understand areas for improvement.

Universal Design for Learning

IDEA requires that students with disabilities have access to the general education curriculum. If students are to learn the general education curriculum, and be assessed on this curriculum, then they must have access to the curriculum. Yet, the most significant barrier for some students to this curriculum is the "fixed medium of presentation" (Hitchcock, Meyer, Rose, & Jackson, 2002, p. 12).

UDL is a theoretical framework developed by the Center for Applied Special Technology (CAST) and is an approach that helps professional educators to meet the challenges of diversity in the classroom. It is intended to guide the development of curricula, instructional practices, and assessments that are flexible and that support all students. The concept was inspired by the universal design movement of architecture, which calls for designs that meet these needs from the onset. Designing structures for individuals with disabilities has resulted in improved usability for everyone.

Educators understand that students have unique and varied interests and learning preferences and that they come to the classroom from varied backgrounds and cultures. A one-size-fits-all curriculum, in which all students are expected to learn in the same way and at the same pace, denies students equal opportunities to learn. UDL helps to break down this barrier to learning through "flexible instructional materials, techniques, and strategies" to address varied learning preferences, different abilities, and wide-ranging interests (CAST, 2008). There are three primary principles to guide UDL: Provide Multiple Means of Representation (the "what" of learning), Provide Multiple Means of Expression (the "how" of learning), and Provide Multiple Means of Engagement (the "why" of learning). Table 3.2 shows the three primary principles with a description and examples.

Differentiated Instruction

Differentiated instruction supports the principles of UDL and aligns well with UDL teaching practices. Differentiated instruction is a promising response to the varied needs and concerns that students bring to the classroom every day (Tomlinson, Brimijoin, & Narvaez, 2008).

Differentiated instruction is a "systematic approach to planning curriculum and instruction for academically diverse learners. It is a way of thinking about the classroom with the dual goals of honoring each student's learning needs and maximizing each student's learning capacity" (Tomlinson & Eidson, 2003, p. 3). According to Tomlinson and Eidson, there are five elements within the classroom that teachers can differentiate.

1. Content: What is taught and how students have access to information and ideas

2. Process: How students come to understand and create meaning of the knowledge and skills of a topic

3. Products: How a student demonstrates what they know, understand, and can do

4. Affect: How students link thought and feeling

5. Learning environment: How the classroom is set up for instruction

Tomlinson (2008) also has identified "nonnegotiables" about how the process of teaching in a differentiated classroom should look; these are shown in Table 3.3, with practices aligned with each requirement.

Teachers should attend to their students' readiness level when they differentiate; the current level of knowledge, understanding, and skill level connected to a particular lesson. Vygotsky (1978), a Russian psychologist, taught that individuals learn best in accordance

Table 3.2. Three primary principles of universal design for learning

Principle	Description	Examples
Multiple Means of Representation (the "what" of learning)	Learners differ in the ways that they perceive and comprehend information and content presented to them. Learning, and the transfer of learning, happens when multiple representations are used because this allows students to make connections within, as well as between, concepts. Providing options for how information is represented is essential, as there is not one means of representation that will be optimal for all learners.	• Use different modalities (visual, tactile and auditory) to provide information • Use visual aids and DVDs • Vary the size of text • Use color for emphasis • Use speech to text technologies • Use methods for visual and auditory cues • Read directions and printed text to the class or use taped versions • Use tactile graphics for key visuals • Use advance organizers • Preteach key concepts. • Anchor instruction in students' prior knowledge • Use analogies and metaphors
Multiple Means of Action and Expression (the "how" of learning)	Learners differ in the ways that they can express what they know. There is no one means of expression that will meet the needs of all students; providing options for expression is essential.	• Use physical manipulatives • Have students "show what they know" through various media (music, art, video, speech, texts, 3D models, storyboards)
Multiple Means of Engagement (the "why" of learning)	Learners vary in the ways in which they can be engaged or motivated to learn. Some students enjoy spontaneity and novelty while others may prefer more structure and routine. There is no one means of representation that will be optimal for all students; providing multiple options for engagement is essential.	• Provide choice • Allow students to participate in creating classroom activities • Have students develop personal academic and behavioral goals • Design authentic, purposeful activities • Engage students in self-evaluation and self-reflection • Allow for experimentation • Provide clear schedules and expectations • Use cooperative learning groups • Provide peer support • Provide continual feedback • Use components of differentiated instruction

Source: Center for Applied Special Technology (2011).

with their readiness to do so. He developed the idea of the zone of proximal development (ZPD) and defined this concept as

> the distance between the actual developmental level as determined by independent problem solving and the level of potential development as determined through problem solving under adult guidance, or in collaboration with more capable peers. (p. 86)

Many education professionals believe that a teacher has a responsibility to give students experiences that are within their zones of proximal development to encourage and advance their learning.

Accommodations, Modifications, and Adaptations

Often the terms *accommodations*, *modifications*, and *adaptations* are used interchangeably, but it is worth noting that accommodations and modifications are two distinct types of

Table 3.3. The nonnegotiables for a differentiated classroom

Nonnegotiable	What is it in practice?
Respecting individuals	• Listening • Asking for input • Giving time • Using humor in a positive way • Highlighting the positive • Learning about and appreciating a person's culture and background • Respectful tasks • Encouraging and expecting personal best • Holding person to high standard • Ensuring a positive learning environment where growth is honored
Owning student success	• Ensuring students know expectations and requirements for success • Expecting success from every student • Continuously monitoring student growth • Adapting instruction • Ensuring access to information, materials, supplies, and supports • Being unwilling to allow students to wait while others "catch up" • Teaching students how to make good choices and wise decisions • Giving useful feedback • Ensuring that students act on the feedback • Finding another way to teach and learn • Being a positive person in the student's life
Building community	• Modeling democracy in the classroom • Speaking about students in a respectful manner • Teaching students to be respectful of others • Giving attention to student strengths • Ensuring everyone is engaged and has a role to play • Helping students experience and understand positive interdependence • Establishing positive shared group experiences • Helping students understand and be aware of common goals with varied routes to meeting the goals • Helping students learn how to support each others' learning
Providing high-quality curriculum	• Teaching for understanding • Teaching for transfer • Insisting on and providing support for consistent growth in high-level thought • Guiding quality discussions on important ideas • Helping students examine varied perspectives • Helping student make connections between the important ideas of the content with their own lives and experience • Supporting students to develop the skills and attitudes necessary for quality work
Assessing to inform instruction	• Systematically observing students at work • Using preassessments to understand students starting points • Using ongoing assessments to monitor student progress and identify needs • Asking students to share interests • Listening and looking for student interests • Asking students about their learning preferences • Observing students in different contexts and modes • Asking students what is working and not working for them • Acting on student suggestions • Using assessments to plan for reteaching, teaching in a different way, extending understanding, developing tasks, modifying time, etc.

(Continued)

Table 3.3.   *(continued)*

Nonnegotiable	What is it in practice?
Implementing flexible classroom routines	• Allowing more time for students who need it • Helping students move ahead who are ready to do so • Using varied seating arrangements to support individual and group work • Systematically planning and using flexible groupings of students based on interests, readiness, learning preference, random assignment, student choice and teacher choice • Ensuring text and supplementary materials at appropriate reading levels • Using varied support systems for access to information • Utilizing whole class, individual, and small-group instruction
Creating varied avenues to learning	• Presenting information in varied modes • Encouraging student exploration and expression of content in varied modes • Providing options for varied learning environments • Assigning tasks at different levels of difficulty and appropriate support to move to the next level • Providing whole-to-part and part-to-whole reminders • Offering clinics or miniworkshops on key skills • Providing interest-based options • Using small-group instruction to target student interests and needs • Using varied homework periodically to consolidate or extend learning • Allowing creative, practical, and analytical exploration of essential content
Sharing responsibility for teaching and learning	• Ensuring student voice for classroom guidelines • Ensuring that students take responsibility for implementation of classroom guidelines • Defining and teaching classroom routines • Debriefing classroom routines often • Guiding students to develop classroom rules • Assigning "teacher roles" to students (passing out materials, establishing due dates for projects, etc.) • Teaching students to play those roles effectively • Asking for student input on how the classroom is working • Teaching for student independence

Source: Adapted from *The Differentiated School: Making Revolutionary Changes in Teaching and Learning,* by Carol Ann Tomlinson, Kay Brimjoin, and Lane Narvaez, Alexandria, VA: ASCD. © 2008 by ASCD. Adapted with permission. Learn more about ASCD at www.ascd.org.

adaptations. Usually *modification* means a change in what is being taught or expected from a student, e.g., simplifying an assignment. An *accommodation* is a change that will help the student overcome or work around his/her disability, e.g., allowing a student who has difficulty writing or typing to give answers orally (National Dissemination Center for Children with Disabilities, 2010).

When planning adaptations, the best place to start is with the creation of the lesson for all learners in the classroom. Figure 3.1 provides the steps for adapting curriculum and instruction.

The first six adaptations allow students to successfully gain knowledge and meet the general education standards, and these may not truly be adaptations, as each should be provided for all students. The adaptations that an educator will use will vary, depending on the needs and goals of the learner. The last three adaptations are individualized for learners with more substantial needs and can be used by educators to assist students in successfully gaining knowledge within the general education classroom (Cole, Horvath, Chapman, Deschenes, Ebeling, & Sprague, 2000). The last three adaptations will be discussed in Chapter 5. Figure 3.2 shows the considerations given to all students as educators design experiences for their students. Table 3.4 shows the connection between UDL, differentiated instruction, and adaptations.

Let's revisit the lives of Brad and Myisha and take a look at how their school lives vary based on the instruction in their classrooms.

Brad and Myisha

Brad sits in the third seat in the third row in his self-contained English class. All the desks are in rows facing the teacher who is in the front of the room, delivering the day's lesson around the topic of their latest novel. The lesson is directly connected to the content standards for Brad's grade level. The teacher uses a PowerPoint presentation to highlight main ideas and asks the students to take notes. Students are provided a note-taking form

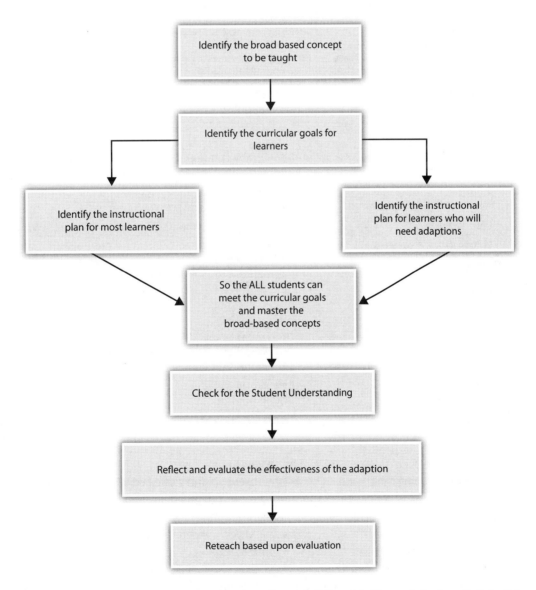

Figure 3.1. Steps to Adaptations to Curriculum and Instruction. (From Cole, C., Horvath, B., Chapman, C., Deschenes, C., Ebeling, D.G., & Sprague, J. [2000]. *Adapting curriculum and instruction in inclusive classrooms: A teacher's desk reference.* [2nd ed.]. Bloomington, IN: Indiana Institute on Disability and Community, Indiana University; reprinted by permission.)

Input	Output	Size
The instructional strategies used to facilitate student learning	The ways learners can demonstrate understanding and knowledge	The length or portion of an assignment, demonstration or performance learners are expected to complete
For example: Using of videos, computer programs, field trips, and visual aids to support active learning.	*For example:* To demonstrate understanding, students write a song, tell a story, design a poster or brochure, or perform an experiment	*For example:* Reduce the length of report to be written or spoken, reduce the number of references needed or the number of problems to be solved.
Time	**Difficulty**	**Level of Support**
The flexible time needed for student learning	The varied skill levels, conceptual levels, and processes involved in learning	The amount of assistance to the learner
For example: Individualize a timeline for project completion or allow more time for test taking.	*For example:* Provide calculators. Tier the assignment so the outcome is the same but with varying degrees of concreteness and complexity.	*For example:* Students work in cooperative groups or with peer buddies, mentors, cross-age tutors or paraeducators.
Degree of Participation	**Modified Goals**	**Substitute Curriculum**
The extent to which the learner is actively involved in the tasks	The adapted outcome expectations within the context of a general education curriculum	The significantly differentiated instruction and materials to meet a learner's identified goal
For example: In a student-written, -directed, and -acted play, a student may play a part that has more physical action rather than numerous lines to memorize.	*For example:* In a written-language activity, a student may focus more on writing some letters and copying words rather than composing whole sentences or paragraphs.	*For example:* In a foreign language class, a student may develop a play or script that uses both authentic language and cultural knowledge of a designated time period, rather than reading paragraphs or directions.

Figure 3.2. Nine types of adaptations. (From Cole, C., Horvath, B., Chapman, C., Deschenes, C., Ebeling, D.G., & Sprague, J. [2000]. *Adapting curriculum and instruction in inclusive classrooms: A teacher's desk reference.* [2nd ed.]. Bloomington, IN: Indiana Institute on Disability and Community, Indiana University; reprinted by permission.)

Table 3.4. Connection between UDL, differentiated instruction, and adaptations

Universal Design	Differentiated Instruction	Adaptations
Multiple means of representation	Differentiated content	Adapt input
	Differentiated affect	Adapt difficulty
	Differentiated learning environment	Substitute curriculum
		Modified goals
		Adapt time
		Adapt size
Multiple means of action and expression	Differentiated products	Adapt output
	Differentiated affect	Adapt time
	Differentiated learning environment	Adapt size
Multiple means of engagement	Differentiated process	Adapt difficulty
	Differentiated affect	Adapt degree of participation
	Differentiated learning environment	Adapt time

to help guide them with this task. The teacher asks questions to the class, and students respond by raising their hands. The teacher presents the same content to all the students. The assignment is given near the end of the period. Students are given a short amount of time to work independently on the assignment and to ask the teacher clarifying questions. The teacher circulates around the classroom, answering questions. The assignment is due the next day.

Myisha's English classroom has small tables where four students sit together. The teacher reads a portion of a chapter from a novel to the class. The lesson for the day is directly connected to the core content standards for Myisha's grade level. The teacher has six essential questions typed on a small piece of paper and hands a different question to each of the tables. She asks them to discuss the questions and to collaboratively create a response. The groups are also asked to create a way to present their response to the rest of the class. The teacher is available for clarifying questions as the students work. Each group then presents its response to the class. Near the end of the period, she passes out an assignment related to the novel chapter and provides choice by offering three options for the activity. The assignment is due the following class period. Students are given an "exit card" (3" × 5" card) and are asked to write one thing they learned from the day's lesson and one thing that they still need to have clarified.

Both Brad and Myisha have instruction that is focused on grade-level content standards. However, for Myisha, there is greater opportunity for her learning needs to be met through the varied instructional strategies.

ACADEMIC RIGOR AND STANDARDS

Since *A Nation at Risk* was published in 1983, there has been increased pressure on schools to increase rigor and raise academic standards for students. Later, No Child Left Behind caused states to take a look at their standards and assessment programs and resulted in high-stakes testing by many states. Willard Daggett (2005) notes that high stakes tests should not become the finish line but rather, "the student's ability to apply high-rigor knowledge in a relevant, real-world setting needs to be the true finish line" (p. 1). Daggett goes on to state that students understand more of what is taught if in fact, they are able to apply the knowledge in a practical and relevant setting. This happens when the roles shift from teacher-centered instruction to student-centered instruction. For example, rather than a teacher sharing new knowledge through lecture, students would use inquiry, experimentation, and investigation to make meaning of the information.

Research by the American Diploma Project and ACT found that the knowledge and skills that high school graduates will need to be successful in college are the same as those they will need to be successful in a job (Achieve, 2004). For both the work force and postsecondary education, a high school graduate must have the English and mathematics knowledge and skills necessary to succeed in entry-level college courses or postsecondary job training/education for a chosen career.

In 2010, the Common Core State Standards were created and have been adopted by a majority of states to ensure that standards are consistent and provide a roadmap for students regardless of where they live. Common core standards define the knowledge and skills students should have within their K–12 education so that they will graduate high school fully prepared for college and careers. The standards

- Aligned with college and work expectations;

- Are clear, understandable and consistent;

- Include rigorous content and application of knowledge through high-order skills;

- Build upon strengths and lessons of current state standards;

- Informed by other top-performing countries, so that all students are prepared to succeed in our global economy and society; and

- Evidence and research-based.

Rigor in the high school curriculum requires that all students be provided the appropriate challenge and the necessary supports to ensure that they meet high standards. These supports include intervention programs and extended learning opportunities. Barriers to access of core standards and differentiated instruction must be eliminated.

Research indicates that successful high schools not only provide rigorous academic coursework, but also are purposeful about providing relevant learning opportunities and meaningful relationships with adults who can support them (Kristin, 2005). Relevant learning experiences include multiple pathways to graduation and linking core content to personal experiences, interests, and connections to the world of work. Educators are beginning to understand the importance of learning experiences that match the needs and interests of the student.

Inquiry-based learning teaches students to seek knowledge and information through questioning. Traditional ways of teaching have discouraged the process of inquiry, relying instead on the teacher to provide facts and students to listen and repeat expected answers. There is a dearth of information and facts readily available to students; the key is to help students make meaning of this information and turn it into useful knowledge. Inquiry-based learning acknowledges the different perspectives and experiences that learners have so that they may have a greater understanding of the world they live in (Teachnology, 2012).

PERSONALIZATION: KNOWING STUDENTS WELL

In most public schools, academic diversity is the norm. All indications are that classrooms are made up of a growing number of students with diverse cultures, sexual orientation, economic backgrounds, exceptionalities, and motivations to "do school."

Clark (2003) defined personalization as

> A learning process in which schools help students assess their own talents and aspirations, plan a pathway toward their own purposes, work cooperatively with others on challenging tasks, maintain a record of their explorations, and demonstrate their learning against clear standards in a wide variety of media, all with the close support of adult mentors and guides. (p. 15)

Teachers must know their students well; they must understand the diversity in learning styles and apply this understanding in the classroom; they must be responsive to the varied backgrounds and cultures of students; they must have the skills to help students apply what they have learned.

Excellent teachers recognize their students' intellectual potential and create environments that support students in reaching their potential. One challenge in creating this environment for learning is finding avenues and the time to know students well, especially as students come from diverse backgrounds and are not all motivated the same way. For high school teachers in particular, this challenge comes with the reality that they may interact with more than 150 students a day.

That said, the research on motivation and student achievement strongly recommends that teachers take the time to deepen their knowledge about individual learners, including their economic backgrounds, ethnic and racial cultures, interests, ways of knowing, and readiness levels (Darling-Hammond & Sykes, 1999; Fullan, Hill, & Crevole, 2006). From a young age, children understand that some people are good at some things, while other people struggle with the same things. They accept that we are not all alike and want to be respected, valued, and nurtured for who they are. Experiences, culture, gender, and genetic codes all affect how and what we learn (Tomlinson, 1999). Teachers who understand this find multiple ways to know their students.

Having a personal relationship with a caring adult who can help students meet high standards academically and socially is also a key concept of quality high schools. This caring adult is often in the form of an advisor or mentor who is the student's advocate throughout high school (Yonezawa, McClure, & Jones, 2012).

Finally, it is essential that schools be communities of learners where character values are fostered through modeling, teaching, expecting, celebrating, and practicing responsibility, hard work, honesty, and kindness (DeRoche & Williams, 2001). Developing the mind and character of students is essential in this global age. Students must be taught to become productive citizens who understand the rights and responsibilities of living in a democracy and are guided to know and pursue what is good and what is worthwhile. Schools cannot simply develop a student's intellectual and academic mind while leaving character formation and development to chance. Character formation helps to shape students attitudes and behaviors that are reflected in the values of integrity, respect, self-discipline, and care.

 ## Understanding Each Student's Unique Story

Both Brad and Myisha have had personalized experiences in school. Brad's connections have been through his special education teacher, who has been his teacher for three years, knows him well, and talks regularly with and understands his family. Myisha has also had strong connections with mentors in high school. She has been a member of the leadership club to mentor younger students and has developed a strong connection to the faculty leader of this group. The faculty leader knows and understands her interests and learning preferences and is an advocate for her with other teachers.

Personalization can happen in a variety of ways in schools, as shown in both Brad and Myisha's examples. However, teachers can become caught up in dealing with student "deficits" and what the student cannot do, versus viewing the student's potential in the context of the possibilities given quality instruction and the necessary supports from a collaborative system. As a former special educator once noted when he began co-teaching an algebra class, "I used to put ceilings on my students, but now, I no longer have ceilings." From the standpoint of personalization, teachers must understand the whole child and advocate for the child, asking the question "How can we make this happen?"

CAREER EXPLORATION

Often children are asked at an early age, "What do you want to be when you grow up?" Many things influence a child's career aspirations. They observe adults in various roles and connect with specific role models. As they get older, students begin to identify interests and skills and begin matching it to their career preferences. Career education promotes the infusion of careers into all subject areas from kindergarten through high school. For young children, a trip to the doctor, seeing the fire truck pass by, watching their teachers, and seeing family members headed to work all provide a glance at the future. When students see the relevance to possible future goals, they are more likely to be motivated to learn the necessary skills to be successful in future settings like college or careers.

Another influence on a child's aspiration comes from the reinforcement of skills and abilities. If a student's strength and interest is using his or her hands to build or take apart items, and the student is given opportunities to explore areas of strength and interests, he or she is more likely to make a connection to a possible career. A focus on career development should permeate the student's entire educational experience. But for some students, these exposures are limited because of a lack of positive role models and the work ethic that they may be exposed to.

Career education can produce a number of outcomes for students, including knowledge and attitudes about careers; orientation about careers; specific skills required to obtain a specific occupation; educational requirements and earning potential, workforce trends, career decisions, and much more (Kochhar-Bryant & Greene, 2009).

Career education as described by Brolin (1995) has four stages: career awareness (elementary /middle), career exploration (middle/high school), career preparation (high school), and career assimilation (high school and beyond). These stages are described as follows.

- **Career awareness.** This stage provides awareness about work, the role of workers, and how students fit into a work-oriented society in later adult years. The focus of this stage is to have students begin to develop work ethic and values; exposure to why people need and want to work; contributions to lifestyle and life choices; exposure to a wide range of careers and jobs across fields; and interpersonal, problem solving, communication, and team skills needed for future careers.

- **Career exploration.** During the career exploration stage, which starts during middle school and extends into high school, students explore their interests, preferences, and abilities as related to their preferred lifestyle and careers. Students are given a variety of opportunities and activities to determine interests, preferences, and abilities. Examples include

  - Participation in simulated activities such as "reality store"
  - Completing learning-style and career-interest inventories
  - Job shadowing and work experiences to narrow career choices
  - Using the Occupational Outlook Handbook or O*Net to identify career categories, educational requirements, earning potential, and market outlook
  - Developing a plan to meet requirements and achieve a "best match" career

- **Career preparation.** Narrowing and confirmation of one career field; student may still explore a range of positions within a related field. Examples include

  - Increasing work experience opportunities to prepare for full-time work in the community; include vocational rehabilitation services as needed
  - Refining interviewing and job seeking skills for work experience positions, and develop job maintenance skills and social/communication skills to keep one's position
  - Identifying potential career advancement and self-advocacy opportunities and strategies

- **Career assimilation.** Participating in real life situations such as job seeking, interviewing, and locating a job, participation in the work place such as the employer activities and support where students apply the work-related skills like problem solving, social skills, task-related skills, and others as all part of career assimilation.

 **Myisha and Brad**

Both Myisha and Brad have had opportunities for career exploration. However, Brad's experiences have supplanted the experiences that other students like Myisha have had. For example, his transition specialist provided the service vs. supporting and supplementing the existing high school services. Because he is in self-contained classes for most of his content classes, he has not had the opportunity to experience the embedded and integrated transition skill activities that other students receive in their general education classes.

INCLUSIVE PRACTICES

The question of *where* a student with a disability should be taught (general education classrooms or separate special education classrooms) has been debated for more than 40 years. The bulk of research on the topic suggests that students with disabilities benefit socially, emotionally, and academically when they are educated with their same age peers in inclusive environments (Barclay et al., 2006; Cole, Waldron, & Madj, 2004; Rea, McLaughlin, & Walther-Thomas, 2002; Waldron and McLeskey, 1998). Access to the general education curriculum, in settings with their peers, is a critical component to the successful transition of students with disabilities. For students with mild disabilities, the greater amount of time a student with disability spends in an inclusive setting, the better their postsecondary outcomes (Grossi & Cole, 2007).

Historically, inclusive practices have been more difficult to establish in secondary schools (Cole & McLeskey, 1997). Educators have suggested that there are many factors

A Look at Inclusive Classrooms

A study by Cole, Waldron, and Madj (2004) investigated the effects of inclusive school settings for students in six school corporations. The results of this investigation reveal that students without disabilities educated in inclusive settings made significantly greater academic progress in mathematics and reading. For students with disabilities, there were no significant differences in reading and math achievement across the comparison groups. However, a review of group means and the percentage of students making comparable or greater than average academic progress when compared to students without disabilities indicates a pattern in favor of inclusive settings. This finding was also supported when considering the academic progress of students with specific disability labels, namely learning disabilities and mild mental handicaps.

A Difference in High Schools.

A 2007 study by Grossi and Cole looked at four high schools in four different school districts. Two of the high schools selected had a history and reputation of including a full range of students with disabilities in the general education classes; and two high schools selected provided a more traditional approach to special education services, with students spending the majority of their instructional time in resource rooms and/or self-contained classrooms. The study found that students spending more time in inclusive settings had more access to the general education curriculum across grade levels (K–12), higher expectations, and more access to extracurricular activities that resulted in higher rates for passing the state proficiency test, higher graduation rates, and improved postschool outcomes (Grossi & Cole, 2007).

that contribute to this, including curriculum demands, school organization, school culture, and the need for students to apply basic skills to learn (McLeskey and Waldron, 2000). Table 3.5 shows factors that impact inclusive practices in secondary schools.

Fortunately, there are many high school examples where students with disabilities are successfully being educated in inclusive settings. In our work with inclusive schools, it has become clear that there are certain key elements that are critical to the successful inclusion of students with disabilities. It isn't enough to simply have students with disabilities physically present in the general education classroom. They must be academically included and engaged in a meaningful way with the curriculum, and they must be socially/emotionally included, with attention given to enhancing student's self-esteem, building capacity for true friendships, implementing a social skills curricula and building a classroom in which individual differences are valued.

What follows is a brief discussion on the essential elements that should be in place to ensure that students with disabilities are supported and successful in inclusive environments.

Unified Systems and Collaboration

It is our belief, based on experience and research, that schools can only meet the challenge of providing both equity and excellence for students by developing a unified system of education and collaborative cultures in which the responsibility and accountability for students is shared (see also Figure 1.1). A unified system is universally designed to support the socioemotional and learning needs of all students. Accountability and responsibility for student learning is shared among all educators, and special education is a seamless part of the general education system. In a unified system, general education interventions and supports as well as special education adaptations, interventions, and supports are provided in the general education setting. This includes an instructional program that incorporates a range of curricula offerings and a variety of instructional strategies; a staff that is culturally and linguistically diverse and trained to meet the needs of

Table 3.5.   Factors that influence inclusionary practices in secondary schools

Factors	Examples
Curriculum demands	• There is an increased emphasis on core academics and a demand to learn content in more depth. • There is conflict between the core academics and providing coursework on career/vocational, life skills, functional living skills, and so on.
The need for students to apply basic skills to learn curricular content	• Some students may lack the basic skills necessary to be successful in core academic areas. • Teachers have a wide range of skills in their classes. • Secondary teachers are often not well equipped to teach basic skills.
School organization	• Teachers often see 150–180 students/day, decreasing their ability to know students well or make the necessary adaptations for student success. • Special education teachers must be well versed in multiple content areas to co-teach and may need to support a large number of classes.
School culture	• The prevailing culture supports content-centered, rather than student-centered orientation. • Most secondary teachers are trained as content specialists and either cannot or are not inclined to make adaptations for students.
Pressures from outside agencies	• Secondary educators are pressured by a wide array of outside influences (colleges, state legislators, businesses etc.). • Accountability for high schools includes drop-out and graduation rates.

Source: McLeskey and Waldron (2000).

the students they serve; opportunities for students to learn self-determination skills and to be engaged in decisions; collaboration among school staff and with community members; family engagement; access to community agency services; a school-wide approach to behavioral issues; a system of accountability that defines success by the learning of every student within each building; a system of transitional services to support students as they move to new settings within the school; and shared resources to meet the needs of all students.

Administrative Support

In our work, we often hear that "administrative leadership made all the difference" in how well inclusive practices are implemented in schools and districts. Administrators help to create the expectation that all students belong and should have access to high-quality instruction with their peers. They help to break down the barriers to inclusion. Administrators help to create the necessary supports and structures for teachers to problem solve and communicate with each other and are instrumental in ensuring that special and general education teaching schedules are flexible and provide time for planning and teaching together. Administrators also model for the school community the importance of educating all students together.

Special Educators' Knowledge of Content Standards

The inclusion of students with disabilities in state and district assessments, as required by No Child Left Behind, has highlighted the need for teachers of special education to have a clear understanding of state and local content standards. In many cases, special education teachers will be supporting students with disabilities in the general education classroom through a co-teaching or consultation model. Therefore, it is imperative that special educators know content standards and are able to collaborate with their general education colleagues to ensure that these standards are being taught.

General Educators' Knowledge and Willingness to Adapt and Differentiate

Adapting curriculum and differentiating instruction are means for supporting a wide range of learners with varied abilities in the same classroom. Demonstrating acceptance and respect for individual learner differences increases the likelihood of student success. In order for classrooms to meet the wide range of learners, teachers must first understand and accept that students differ in important ways and that this will require teachers to think about new ways of teaching and learning (Cole et al., 2000). General education teachers can make a difference in the lives of all students when they have the knowledge and skills to differentiate and adapt instruction (Hoover & Patton, 2005; Kern, Bambara, & Fogt, 2002).

Academic Support Programs

Some students who are included in the general education program may need some additional support beyond the general education classroom. Examples include study skills classes, resource programs for reteaching and preteaching, guided study halls, peer buddies, homework clubs, student advisory periods, group or individual counseling, and social skills programs. Academic support programs should *reinforce and supplement* skills addressed in the general education classroom, not *replace* the instruction in the general education classroom.

Shared Vision and Definition of Inclusion

Organizational change literature is clear that in order to create and sustain change, there is a need for a desirable vision for a future state (Senge, 2006; Burello, Lashley, & Beatty, 2001). Vision and mission statements in districts and schools should be inclusive of all students and should be shared by all staff. In addition, all of the school community should have a shared definition of inclusion as programs and practices are developed, implemented, and sustained. Without this shared knowledge, misunderstandings and conflicts can develop. In his testimony to the President's Commission on Excellence in Special Education (2002), Wayne Sailor provided an extensive and comprehensive description of the various terms used over the years to describe inclusive practices as described in Table 3.6.

Ongoing Professional Development

In order for educators to have the knowledge and skills to implement inclusive programs, they must be provided with the appropriate professional development. If we expect students with and without disabilities to learn together, we must also provide opportunities for general and special educators to learn together. The professional development should be ongoing and should follow the standards outlined for quality professional development.

Table 3.6. Historical inclusion definition terms

Term	Dates	Definition	Features
Inclusion	First appeared in literature around 1990	The placement of students with disabilities in the general education classroom	• Students who attend their home school. • Age-appropriate placements • Special education supports in the general education classroom
Full inclusion	Around 1992	Came to stand for a kind of no-exceptions policy arguing for full-time participation in age-appropriate, general education classrooms for all IDEA-served students, no matter how extensive or significant their disabilities	• Advanced by those in special education community associated with students with significant disabilities • Grounded in the philosophy of social participation and development • Arguments were based on civil rights
Inclusive education	Around 1992	Called for a "home-base" placement of all students as members of a general education classroom but left open opportunities for students to be taught in other environments within the school and in the community	• Had a school-wide rather than classroom-based focus • Argued against placement of students with disabilities in special classes • Accepted the possibility of removal for those periods during which the IEP team determines that the student is unlikely to derive educational benefits from participation, regardless of in-class support
Universal design	Early 2000s	Educational programs become multidisciplinary team-generated practices focused within schools to enhance access to the general education curriculum and maximize outcomes from the general curriculum and its standards by all students, including those with disabilities	• Application of high standards and rigor for all students • Grounded in the literature on standards-based reform

Source: Sailor (2002).

This means that the one-stop workshop cannot be the prevailing experience that teachers have as they implement inclusive practices.

SUMMARY

In order to provide quality transition services, a foundation must be laid that includes the components that we have discussed in this chapter. Clearly, success for students is dependent on access to quality instruction in an inclusive environment that provides high expectations and personalization. The role for special educators is to provide flexible, ongoing support and resources within the context of the general education system.

FOR FURTHER INFORMATION

CAST (http://www.cast.org)

    Articles, strategies, and practical material for implementing UDL

Common Core State Standards Initiative (http://www.corestandards.org)

    Includes full listing of the standards, rationale, and some guidance for implementation

McREL's Classroom Instruction That Works (http://www.mcrel.org/citw)

    A collection of products is invaluable to classroom teachers working with diverse groups of learners

Council for Exceptional Children's Teaching and Learning Center (http://www.cec.sped.org/Content/NavigationMenu/NewsIssues/TeachingLearningCenter/default.htm)

    Provides articles and strategies on a variety of topics related to inclusive teaching practices. The main CEC web site also includes extensive information about policy.

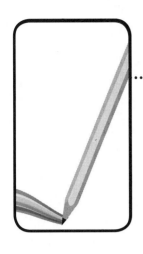

4

Bringing It Together

Good Transition and Good Instructional Practices

Our intent in Chapters 2 and 3 was to provide an overview of transition and instructional practices that promote good postschool outcomes within a unified system of education. In this chapter, we will use the conceptual framework described in Chapter 1 to show how to bring together quality transition services and quality educational practices.

One premise of the conceptual framework is that transition services are not reserved for students with IEPs. All students, with and without disabilities, require transition services and activities to help them reach their postschool goals. While some students need more unique supports and services, all students can benefit when there is a good foundation of educational practices and a good foundation of transition services and activities. Also, quality educational practices in general must not start in high school but be a part of the entire K–12 system.

We often get the question, "How can I provide transition services and conduct transition assessments when the student is spending the majority or all of his or her time in the general education classroom?" To address conducting transition services in a unified system, there are some guidelines.

- Transition services and activities should supplement, not supplant, what is already occurring in the general education environment.

- Teachers must be "purposeful and deliberate" in identifying transition skills and activities, including transition assessments, that will help inform the student and the team about transition planning and the transition IEP.

- Since transition services are a coordinated set of activities in which teachers must be "purposeful and deliberate," special educators must understand the general education curriculum and build relationships with general educators to ensure communication and coordination of services and activities.

 **Myisha, Brad, and Their Friend Carlos**

When Myisha and Brad participated in the high school orientation program, which occurs for all incoming freshman, they met Carlos. Carlos does not have an IEP. The three of them shared their fears and anxieties, as well as their excitement about entering high school. Myisha was concerned about finding and opening her locker. Brad and Carlos were concerned about making it to all their classes on time because the school was so large and spread out.

In activities with the guidance counselor, Carlos talked about coming from a large family. His parents did not go college, but they have big dreams for him. They want him to have choices about his future life. Carlos has done well academically through his first eight years of school. The discussion with his counselor was the first time Carlos began to believe that he could attend college. His four-year plan was set up to include college prep courses and electives in music, which is a strong interest and talent.

Through the stories of Brad, Myisha, and Carlos, we will demonstrate how general education is the foundation for providing transition services that lead to successful post-secondary outcomes for students with and without disabilities. This chapter will show how our three students progress through the high school years by using our conceptual framework, applying the practices described in Chapters 2 and 3. Additional examples, resources and forms to be used for everyday purposes are included in an appendix at the end of this chapter.

THE UNIVERSAL LEVEL OF TRANSITION SERVICES

Quality high schools and quality transition services for all students serve as the foundation of our conceptual framework. General educators are key partners in universal level transition activities. There are many aspects of the general education assessment and instruction process that can inform transition planning. We will look at each of the elements of quality instruction, academic rigor and standards, personalization, career exploration, and inclusive practices and show how transition activities are embedded in each element.

Quality Instruction

How do I identify classroom activities that can be used as a part of transition assessment and the transition IEP and planning process?

Within a classroom with quality instruction, there are many elements that can link to the necessary transition skills and services for students to be successful in post-school settings.

Curriculum content

First, it is important that the special education teacher understand what is being taught in the general education classroom. For example, what units are being taught, what are the standards and the related content, and how do these tie to individual student programs? It will be important for special educators to develop or find structures that will enable a collaborative partnership with their general education colleagues. This can happen through a co-teaching partnership, consultation, using technology to share units, communication with a paraeducator, short informal conversations during the school day, or quick observations of various activities related to the unit. Students can also be a good source of information regarding what is being taught. Once special educators know the content and units, they can begin to identify what transition skills are being taught and if the information can be used as part of transition assessments. See Appendix A for unit examples with related transition skills at the end of each unit.

Quality Instruction and Transition Skills Example

Grade 11: U.S. History: Students are introduced to a unit of study that examines American history through the lens of civil rights. Students are introduced to key social movements that have had a great impact on the nation's history: women's suffrage movement, African American civil rights movement, Asian American civil rights movement, and the disabilities rights movement. Over the course of the unit, students choose one movement to research, investigating the associated injustices, strategies, and achievements. After demonstrating their understanding of the past in the form of a case study, students apply what they have learned to current-day civil rights issues, raising public awareness and promoting action.

Transition skills: Empowerment, self-determination, self-awareness, self-advocacy, teamwork

Knowing Your Students

Teachers in a good differentiated classroom will purposefully spend time getting to know their students, preassessing their skills and creating learning profiles to inform instruction. Activities focused on getting to know the students will provide a wealth of information that can be used as part of the transition assessment and student profile.

There are many examples of tools and strategies that teachers use to get to know their students.

- Learning profiles (e.g., the Preferred Ways of Learning form [see Figure 4.1] and Figure 4.2)

- Learning inventories

- Interest inventories (e.g. Figure 4.3 or the Student Interest Survey Questions to Pose form [see Figure 4.4])

- Reflective writing (e.g., the Self-Reflection Activity form [see Figure 4.5])

- Observing students

- Asking parents, "Tell me about your child"

- Asking students to respond to the questions, "What helps you to be successful in school?" or "What can I do to make this a great learning year for you?" (e.g., Working Preferences form in Figure 4.6)

- Interviews

- Visuals: Collages, show and tell (e.g., the In-Common Quilt form [Figure 4.7] and Figure 4.8)

- Timed and untimed writing samples

- Journaling

A Student's Voice

Educational Leadership Online interviews students to understand "What Helps Us Learn." Tune in to hear honest, emotional comments from high school students with disabilities talk about how important it is for teachers to connect with their class and learn something about each student (http://bcove.me/lmkd8vxz).

Preferred Ways of Learning: Auditory/Visual/Kinesthetic

Directions: In each section, check the statements that apply to you. Leave the others blank.

Section A

1. ___ If I need to spell a word correctly, I write it down to see if it "looks" right.
2. ___ I can remember names if I see them written on nametags.
3. ___ I enjoy reading books and looking at the pictures.
4. ___ I would prefer to read the directions or look at the illustrations before beginning a project.
5. ___ To remember what my teacher says in class, it helps me to take notes.
6. ___ I usually write down all of my assignments to help me remember them.
7. ___ A good way for me to practice vocabulary words would be to use flashcards.
8. ___ I like my desk and locker to be organized.
9. ___ I can sit still to watch TV or work on the computer for a long time.
10. ___ I understand things better when I read them than when I listen to them.
11. ___ I like for my parents to make a list of the chores I need to do rather than just tell me.
12. ___ I can picture things easily in my mind.

Section B

1. ___ If I hear someone's name, I remember it easily.
2. ___ I prefer to listen to a book on tape rather than read it myself.
3. ___ I can pay attention and remember easily when my teacher reads aloud to us.
4. ___ I use jingles and songs to help me memorize things.
5. ___ If I were lost, I would stop and ask someone for directions rather than look at a map.
6. ___ When reading, I can best remember a story if we have a class discussion about it.
7. ___ I remember songs after hearing them only a couple of times.
8. ___ I often read and study by repeating information aloud to myself.
9. ___ I am distracted by background noise (like pencil tapping) when I am taking a test.
10. ___ I like to study for tests by having someone quiz me aloud.
11. ___ I like to talk and listen.
12. ___ I work math story problems by talking through them aloud.

Section C

1. ___ It is hard for me to pay attention when I must sit still for a whole class period.
2. ___ I enjoy sports and being active.
3. ___ I count on my fingers or with other objects when I do math problems.
4. ___ My favorite classes are those where I can move around a lot.
5. ___ I would almost always choose to play outside rather than sit inside and read a book or listen to tapes.
6. ___ I have a hard time staying neat and organized.
7. ___ I am good at skills like walking on a balance beam, serving a volleyball or playing baseball.
8. ___ I prefer to learn a new activity by being shown how to do it rather than reading about it or listening to a tape about it.

Figure 4.1. Preferred ways of learning: Auditory/visual/kinesthetic. (*Source:* RapidBI, 2007.)

In *Teaching Transition Skills in Inclusive Schools* by Teresa Grossi, Ph.D., and Cassandra M. Cole, Ed.D.
Copyright © 2013 by Paul H. Brookes Publishing Co., Inc. All rights reserved.

(continued)

9. __ I would like to act out stories rather than talk about them.

10. __ I have a good sense of balance and rhythm.

11. __ I can learn new dance steps or athletic skills after only trying them a few times.

12. __ I would like to study my multiplication tables by saying them in rhythm while I jumped rope.

TOTAL NUMBER OF CHECKS IN SECTION A   _____

TOTAL NUMBER OF CHECKS IN SECTION B   _____

TOTAL NUMBER OF CHECKS IN SECTION C   _____

A. If your highest total is in section A, you are likely a **VISUAL** learner. You remember best by using your eyes.

B. If your highest total is in section B, you are likely an **AUDITORY** learner. You remember best by using your ears.

C. If your highest total is in section C, you are likely an **ACTIVE/KINESTHETIC** learner. You need movement or activity while you study to remember best.

I am strongest as a _____ learner.

My second area of strength is as a _____ learner.

AVK Modalities: Our Sensory Preferences

Visual

If you prefer this modality, you tend to process information better when it is supplied in the form of pictures, diagrams, graphs and so on. You probably say "I see" or "I get the picture," when you are at workshops or other learning environments. Visual people like handouts and often take good notes with "mind maps" of ideas and little diagrams.

Characteristics: Neat and tidy, speak quickly, good planning and organization, observant especially of environmental detail, good speller—can see the words in your mind, remember what has been seen rather than heard, memorize by visual association, may forget verbal instructions, prefer reading to being read to, make doodles during conversations

Auditory

If this is your preferred modality, you will catch yourself saying "I hear you" or "That sounds like a good idea." You will learn best by listening to conversations or presentations. Taking notes will probably get in the way of your learning.

Characteristics: If this is our preferred modality, you will learn by listening, speak in rhythmic patterns, talk to yourself, easily distracted by noise, move their lips and say the words as they read, enjoy reading aloud, good at repeating music, better at telling than writing down, eloquent speakers, talkative and enjoy discussions, can spell out loud rather than writing down.

Kinesthetic

If this is your preferred modality, you likely learn by hands on activities and working within groups. You will probably catch yourself building models or moving objects around as you explain abstract concepts.

Characteristics: If this is your preferred modality, you likely learn by manipulating, want to act things out, touch people to get attention, memorize by walking and seeing, like to move, remember geographic locations because you have been there, use action words, like books with a strong plot, enjoy involved games.

Goal: Research and present an argument on 1 of the 3 topics: blocking specific web sites in school, drug testing, or uniforms in schools

Teacher: Mr. Hardy   Subject: English (persuasive writing)   Standards (Common Core):

Learning Element	Students Strengths	Students Needs	Students Preferences/ Interests
Learning "what"	Dakota: Extensive vocabulary Jeremy: Thorough knowledge of debating skills	Jason: Limited English proficiency Natalie: Low vision Ashley: Poor reading comprehension skills	Dakota, Jake, Mandy, Kyle, Heather: Love using web and computers Ryan, Nicole and Michael: Prefer hands-on activities Elizabeth, Ashley, Jason: Works well with a lot of structure
Learning "how"	Jake: Excellent research skills and technology resources Mandy: Good presentation skills Kyle: Good writing skills	Nicole: Poor organizational skills Ryan: Difficulty writing Michael: Difficulty writing	
Learning "why"	James: Very confident; high self-esteem Elizabeth: Good social skills/collaborative groups Heather: Doesn't give up, good work ethic	Ryan: Easily discouraged and lacks self-confidence Nicole: Easily distracted, a little "too" social Ashley: Dealing with a lot of personal issues	Elizabeth and James: Need to be challenged

Figure 4.2. Class learning profile. (*Source:* Adapted from *Teaching Every Student in the Digital Age: Universal Design for Learning*, by David Rose and Anne Meyer, Alexandria, VA: ASCD. © 2002 by ASCD. Adapted with permission. Learn more about ASCD at www.ascd.org.)

What Do We Have in Common?

Each group member will need a 5" x 7" card. Once cards are distributed, give the groups the following directions:

1. Put your name in the center of your card.
2. In the upper left corner, write the name of your favorite video game.
3. In the upper right corner, write down what your best subject is in school.
4. In the lower left corner, write your favorite after-school activity.
5. In the lower right corner, write the type and name of your pet.

When everyone finishes, they are to find one or two people who have something similar written in the left hand corner of the card and visit for a few minutes. Repeat with the upper right corner, lower left corner and lower right corner information. No two people can be in the same group more than once.

Getting to Know You: Using the Venn Diagram or Moving Around the Room

Divide students into groups of three or four and provide each group with a large sheet of paper on which to write. Each member of the group should be given a colored marker in different colors. Each student should then draw a Venn diagram with an oval for each student. When this is done, the students in each group should begin discussion of their similarities and differences. You may want to prompt the groups by getting them started with questions about favorite music, number of siblings, favorite after-school activity, and so forth. After the discussion, they are to fill in the diagram showing their similarities and differences.

Alternative: An alternative to the Venn Diagram is to choose specific questions the students have to respond to and have them move to a corner of the room to look at similarities and differences. For example, students who have only one sibling go to the right lower corner of room; students who have two siblings go to the lower left hand corner; students with three siblings to lower right corner of room; and students who have four or more siblings go lower left corner of the room.

Other questions could be: type of video game, types of food, pets, and so forth.

Figure 4.3. Student interests—interactive activities. ("What Do We Have in Common?" activity adapted from University of California at Berkeley Division of Student Affairs [n.d.].)

Student Interest
Survey Questions to Pose

1. What is your favorite book from childhood?

2. What is the farthest point you've traveled away from home?

3. What is a recent movie you enjoyed, and what did you like about it?

4. What is your favorite place to be and why?

5. What is your favorite food?

6. What is your favorite kind of music?

7. What is your favorite sport?

8. To what organizations, teams, or clubs do you belong?

9. Name someone you admire and tell why.

10. What are two common activities you do after getting home from school?

11. What is a responsibility you have?

12. What wish do you have for someone else?

13. What do you want to do for a career?

14. What is something about which you daydream?

15. What is something about which you are curious?

16. What would the title of a book about your life be?

17. If you could go back two years ago, what advice would you give yourself?

18. Describe yourself as a friend.

19. Describe your best friend.

20. What should I know about you to teach you well?

Figure 4.4. Student interest survey questions to pose.

Self-Reflection Activity

Students respond in journals, with exit-card probes, in small-group discussion, or on a graffiti wall.

1. If I could do anything, I'd . . .

2. Usually, when I have free time, I . . .

3. My hobbies are . . .

4. At school I like to . . .

5. The types of things we do in class that I really like are . . .

6. I get bored in class when . . .

7. I wish my teachers would . . .

8. I am uncomfortable when people ask me to . . .

9. Do you like to work alone or in a group? Why?

10. School would be better if . . .

Figure 4.5. Self-reflection activity.

Working Preferences

1. Do you like quiet or noise (music, TV…) when you study? Quiet   Noise

2. Where do you prefer to work on assignments? (on the floor, at a desk, on a computer)

3. If you are not able to complete something, it is because…

    you forgot.   it's boring.   you got distracted.   you need help.

4. Where do you like to sit in class?

    Near the door   In the front   In the back   By a wall   By a window

5. Do you like to work with a partner? Why or why not?

6. When are you most alert? In the afternoon? In the morning? In the evening?

7. What classes do you enjoy most and why?

8. Describe where, when, and how you study.

9. If you have an assignment due in two weeks, how do you plan to make sure it is completed on time?

10. If something is new to you, do you: Like to have it explained? Like to read about it? Like to just try it?
    Like to watch a DVD/demonstration?

Figure 4.6. Working preferences.

Teaching Transition Skills in Inclusive Schools by Teresa Grossi, Ph.D., and Cassandra M. Cole, Ed.D.

In-Common Quilt

We all know the importance of facilitating relationships in the classroom. Students benefit from structured opportunities to get to know one another. Discovering commonalities with peers goes a long way to building relationships and appreciating differences. You could also teach the attributes of a square, the use of grids, meaning of rows and columns, multiplication, and fractions.

Grade level: K–adult

Objective: Students discover things they have in common with peers

Materials: Colored paper squares, markers, crayons, colored pencils or other objects that might decorate the quilt or represent ideas

Groupings: Students can work in groups of three or more. If you had 24 students in class, you could create eight different quilts.

Directions: Students find two things that they have in common with each member of the group. They also discover something that is unique to them. A visual probably works best.

In-Common Quilt	Sandi	Angela	Max	Barb
Sandi	In band	Lives downtown	Hang out on holidays with mutual friends	In same class from kindergarten through 6th grade
Angela	Parents went to college together	100% Dutch – It's true!!	Marathons	Three brothers and one sister
Max	Moved around a lot	Went to middle school together	Class president	Can dunk a basketball
Barb	Likes to be involved in school activities	Ice cream is favorite dessert	Plays basketball	Parachuted

Figure 4.7. In-common quilt.

From Center on Education and Lifelong Learning at Indiana Institute on Disability and Community (2012). In-common quilt. Bloomington, IN: Author; adapted by permission. In *Teaching Transition Skills in Inclusive Schools* by Teresa Grossi, Ph.D., and Cassandra M. Cole, Ed.D. (2013, Paul H. Brookes Publishing Co., Inc.)

Figure 4.8. Myisha's sample of "Nobody Like Me" activity. (From Indiana Institute on Disability and Community [2012]. Nobody's like me activity. Bloomington, IN: Author; reprinted by permission.)

These strategies can give both general and special educators a great deal of insight into their students and will also help the student better understand him or herself. Teachers should coordinate their plans so students do not experience duplication of the same activities.

 ## Getting to Know Myisha in Her Science Class

In Myisha's science class, her teacher conducted the "Nobody's Like Me" activity (Figure 4.8; a blank form is also in the appendix at the end of this chapter) with her students. Based on the questions, you can see that Myisha wants to make sure people know she is very capable with support and encouragement (question #6), is worried about her future (question #8), and really does not like being identified with special education (question #4).

All of this information can be used as a part of the ongoing transition assessment process and included in transition IEP. It is important to use a variety of tools to assess different aspects to contribute to the bigger student profile.

Preassessment

Preassessment activities will help the teacher determine the appropriate level of instruction for students. Preassessment is a way to determine what students know about a topic prior to instruction and should be used frequently in all curricular areas to make decisions about student strengths and needs to make decisions about flexible groups and to understand which students are ready for advanced instruction or need additional supports. Information coming from these assessments can be used in the development and/or monitoring of the transition IEP annual goals. For example, when writing the present level of academic and function performance, information gathered from these preassessment techniques may help show where the student is performing as related to grade-level standards. For example, an English teacher may try to determine where his or her students are performing regarding research skills. Table 4.1 lists several preassessment options that can be used with a class.

Cooperative Learning

Cooperative learning is a strategy teachers can use to give students opportunities to develop the skills necessary to work as a part of a team, to complete a project, and to interact socially with peers. From a transition skill perspective, cooperative learning supports many of the skills required in a work environment, such as teamwork, meeting timelines, and social skills. Cooperative learning assessments could be provided to the special education teacher as additional information on individual students and transition planning process. The Collaborative Rubric form (see Figure 4.9) offers an assessment tool for teachers to use to rate students as they participate in cooperative learning activities. It can also be used as a self-assessment by students.

Helping Students Manage Data

Advanced organizers, assignment notebooks and planners are other examples of classroom activities that can support transition. These tools help students learn how to manage assignments, due dates, meetings, and work completion. Organizational skills and time management are often annual goals for students with disabilities because they are barriers to making progress in the general education curriculum, and they are also valuable skills for postsecondary education, employment, and independent living. These skills must be taught directly, in a content area classroom or a study skills/resource classroom, or in multiple settings.

Self-Reflection

Finally, instruction that provides multiple means for students to show what they know and understand teaches students self-determination skills, facilitates sifting through choices, helps them understand their own learning style, and affords them a chance to better understand their own strengths, preferences, interests,

Table 4.1. Preassessment options: Every pupil response techniques

Technique	Description
Choral response	Students give a choral response to a whole class question. This allows the teacher to determine if most students understand a concept.
Clothesline	Students move to a place in a human line that most closely matches their level of understanding. The line is a continuum, with the beginning of the line indicating no understanding of a concept and the opposite end of the line indicating a high level of understanding.
Fist of five	Students respond to a whole class question by showing the number of fingers that corresponds to their level of understanding (one being the lowest; five, the highest).
Four corners	Students move to a corner of the room that most closely matches their level of understanding. Previously, the teacher must label each corner of the room with a word or phrase that describes the learner's level of understanding.
Individual response boards	Students will use white boards or think pads to respond to a question posed by the teacher. The students hold up their answers for the teacher to check, or the teacher can circulate the class to check individual responses.
Signal cards	Students use a card to indicate their level of understanding of a concept. Cards may be labeled as follows. • Red, yellow, and green • Yes/No • True/False • Negative/Positive • Stop; I'm lost / Slow down; I'm getting confused / Full steam ahead • Happy face, straight face, or sad face
Speedometer	Students think of a speedometer going from 0 to 100 miles per hour. They then lay one arm on top of the other with hands touching elbows. Students should raise the arm that is on top, stopping at a point between 0 and 100 mph to indicate their level of understanding, with 100 mph designating complete understanding.
Thumbs up	Students respond to a whole class question by putting thumbs up if they fully understand a concept, thumbs down if they do not understand, and thumbs to the side to indicate some area of confusion.
Windshield	Students should respond "muddy," "buggy," or "clear" when the teacher asks them to describe their level of understanding. Previously, the teacher explains that "muddy" means the windshield is plastered with mud and the destination is not visible, indicating little or no understanding. "Buggy" means that some debris is littering the windshield, or partial understanding. A clear windshield indicates a high level of understanding.
Entrance card or warm-up	Prior to a lesson, students respond in writing to a question or set of questions posed by the teacher.
Exit card	Students respond in writing to a prompt or question posed by the teacher at the conclusion of a lesson.
Journal/free write	Students write what they know about a given topic. The writing may be timed.
KWL chart	Students complete a graphic organizer specifying what they already know about a topic and what they want or expect to learn. After the lesson, students record what they have learned.
Matching	Students match vocabulary terms to the definitions.
Most difficult first	Students are given the option of completing the most difficult questions or problems first to determine if additional practice is needed.
Observation	Students complete a task as the teacher observes, takes notes, or records progress using a checklist.
Pre- or posttest	Students complete an assessment to demonstrate background knowledge on a topic.
Word sort	Students sort terms into groups using categories chosen by the teacher or created by the students.

Collaborative Rubric

Category	Exemplary	Proficient	Partially Proficient	Unsatisfactory	Points ___/3
Focus on the Task and Participation	3 points	2 points	1 point	0 points	
	Consistently stays focused on the task and what needs to be done. Very self-directed.	Focuses on the task and what needs to be done most of the time. Other group members can count on this person.	Focuses on the task and what needs to be done some of the time. Other group members must sometimes remind this person to keep on task.	Rarely focuses on the task and what needs to be done. Lets others do the work.	
	A true team member who contributes a lot of effort, and encourages and supports the efforts of others in the group.	A strong group member who tries hard.	Sometimes a satisfactory group member who does what is required.	Sometimes chooses not to participate and does not complete assigned tasks.	
Dependability and Shared Responsibility	Consistently punctual for group meetings, turns in all work on time.	Usually punctual for group meetings, turns in most work on time.	Sometimes late for group meetings, frequently turns in work after the deadline.	Late for all or most group meetings, misses all deadlines for turning in work.	
	Follows through on assigned tasks and does not depend on others to do the work, responsibility for tasks is shared evenly.	Follows through on most assigned tasks.	Does not follow through on most assigned tasks and sometimes depends on others to do the work.	Seldom or never follows through on assigned tasks. Depends on others to do all of the work.	
Listening, Questioning and Discussing	Respectfully listens, interacts, discusses and poses questions to all members of the team during discussions and helps direct the group in reaching consensus.	Respectfully listens, interacts, discusses and poses questions to others during discussions.	Has some difficulty respectfully listening and discussing, and tends to dominate discussions.	Has great difficulty listening, argues with teammates, and is unwilling to consider other opinions. Impedes group from reaching consensus.	
Research and Information Sharing	Routinely gathers research and shares useful ideas when participating in the group discussion. Defends/ rethinks ideas relating to the group's project goals.	Usually provides useful research and ideas when participating in the group discussion.	Sometimes provides useful research and ideas when participating in the group discussion.	Rarely provides useful research or ideas when participating in the group discussion.	
Problem Solving	Actively looks for and suggests solutions to problems.	Refines solutions suggested by others.	Does not suggest or refine solutions, but is willing to try out solutions suggested by others.	Does not try to solve problems or help others solve problems.	

Figure 4.9. Collaborative rubric.

From Franker, K. (2007). Collaboration rubric. Menomonie, WI: University of Wisconsin–Stout; reprinted by permission. In *Teaching Transition Skills in Inclusive Schools* by Teresa Grossi, Ph.D., and Cassandra M. Cole, Ed.D. (2013, Paul H. Brookes Publishing Co., Inc.)

Collaborative Rubric *(continued)*

Group/ Partner Teamwork	3 points	2 points	1 point	0 points	___/3
	Consistently makes necessary compromises to accomplish a common goal.	Usually makes necessary compromises to accomplish a common goal.	Occasionally makes compromises to accomplish a common goal, and sometimes helps keep the group working well together.	Rarely makes compromises to accomplish a common goal and has difficulty getting along with other group members	
	Always has a positive attitude about the task(s) and the work of others.	Usually has a positive attitude about the task(s) and the work of others.	Occasionally is publicly critical of the task(s) or the work of other members of the group.	Is often negative and publicly critical of the task(s) or the work of other members of the group.	
	All team members contributed equally to the finished project.	Assisted group/ partner in the finished project.	Finished individual task but did not assist group/partner during the project	Contributed little to the group effort during the project.	
	Performed all duties of assigned team role and contributed knowledge, opinions, and skills to share with the team. Always did the assigned work.	Performed nearly all duties of assigned team role and contributed knowledge, opinions, and skills to share with the team. Completed most of the assigned work.	Performed a few duties of assigned team role and contributed a small amount of knowledge, opinions, and skills to share with the team. Completed some of the assigned work.	Did not perform any duties of assigned team role and did not contribute knowledge, opinions, or skills to share with the team. Relied on others to do the work.	
				Total Points	___/18

From Franker, K. (2007). Collaboration rubric. Menomonie, WI: University of Wisconsin–Stout; reprinted by permission. In *Teaching Transition Skills in Inclusive Schools* by Teresa Grossi, Ph.D., and Cassandra M. Cole, Ed.D. (2013, Paul H. Brookes Publishing Co., Inc.)

and support needs. The following are examples of the multiple ways students can show what they know and can be used across the grade levels. Even when content is not directly related to transition skills, giving students the opportunity to make choices like this helps build skills they will need for adult life.

Self-reflection is a good way for students to evaluate their own performance and growth. Figure 4.10 shows an example of a self-reflection exercise Brad did after his history unit. Self-reflection helps promote transition skills such as self-advocacy, self-awareness of what learning strategies work, and self-determination. For group work, students can also reflect on their contributions to the team. See the appendix at the end of the chapter for blank individual and group self-reflection forms.

Finding Transition Skills and Assessments in the General Education Classroom

In U.S. history class, Carlos and Myisha chose to look at the African American civil rights movement. Brad decided to look at the disability rights movement. The preassessments to determine learning barriers indicated that Carlos and Brad would need supports in gathering and organizing information. Even though Carlos does not have an IEP, the supports provided to Brad were also beneficial to him. By the end of this unit, Brad had more insight into his own learning struggles and the importance of self-advocacy. He also began to understand that there were many successful individuals who had a disability. The unit provided all students in the class with an opportunity to develop their researching, time management, and organizational skills. Because the unit culminated with student presentations, the students also had to learn to speak in front of their peers. This was especially difficult for Brad because he had not given many presentations in his past schooling experiences or been in many large classes.

All three students completed a student self-evaluation reflection form. Myisha and Brad's special education teacher used the preassessment information and the self-reflection form as a part of transition assessment information. All three students used this information as a part of their portfolios.

Name _____ **Brad** _____   Class ___ **U.S. History** _____

Give a brief description of the project or activity you have completed.	**What did you like about this project or activity? What were you able to do well?**
• Civil rights movement • Looked at disability rights movement • Researched the movement • Created a presentation about what I learned and what it meant for today	• I got to choose what civil rights movement I wanted to explore. • I got to choose how I presented the information.
What did you not like about this project or activity? What problems did you have? Why?	**What did you learn about yourself? Strengths, interests, preferences, and needs.**
• It was hard speaking in front of the class. • It was a little hard getting things done on time. • There was a lot of information. I had to figure out what was important and what I should use.	• The biggest thing I learned was there are a lot of successful people who have learning disabilities like me. • I learned I need to practice speaking in front of people more, and once I got over the nervousness, I did OK. • I learned I need to use my accommodations and advocate for myself.

Figure 4.10. Student self-assessment and reflections.

Why is my student not passing the class?

Hypothesis: The student isn't turning in assignments.

Why is my student not turning in homework?

Hypothesis:
-Student works evenings.
-Student doesn't have home support.
-Student has poor time management and organizational skills.
-Student doesn't know the content.

What are the resources we need to have in place for the student to complete assignments and pass the class?

Possible solutions:
-Reduce work hours
-Use resource time for direct instruction
-Adapt the homework assignments
-Teach time management and organizational skills
-Provide a mentor or tutor

Figure 4.11. Sample process for identifying barriers to student learning.

Academic Rigor and Standards

How to I support students who really struggle to keep up and meet the requirements of the general education courses?

In Chapter 3 we discussed the increase in rigor and academic standards for students and the adoption of the Common Core State Standards across the country. Access to academic rigor and general education standards is a key factor for students to achieve positive postsecondary outcomes, but many students will need supports to fully engage with the curriculum. An important step in transition planning is to identify the support needs of students to ensure they meet their postsecondary goals. It requires teachers to move from believing that the student cannot succeed to asking the question "What supports are necessary for the student *to* succeed?" Teachers must have a good understanding of the barriers that may be keeping a student from being successful and how to overcome them (see Figure 4.11).

If it is determined that a student requires some skill-based direct instruction, the support should not replace instruction in the general education classroom. If a student has a study skills or resource class, these skills should be explicitly taught in this context. Skills such as time management, organization, learning strategies, and self-advocacy are critical to future success in college and careers. In addition, some of these strategies can be embedded and taught within the context of the general education classroom. This kind of skill-based support applies to students with and without disabilities.

 ## Identifying Brad's Barriers

The U.S. history class was the first high school general education core content class for Brad. He had encouragement from his counselor and the history teacher to consider taking this class. In past IEP meetings, it had always been suggested that he would struggle with the content and would not be able to keep up. However, the guidance counselor asked the question "What supports would Brad need to be successful in U.S. history?" The team discussed with Brad the types of supports that would help. They decided that Brad needed accommodations for reading, an adult to monitor his planner, peer support for note taking and resource time if necessary. To everyone's surprise, Brad did above-average work. When exposed to high expectations and curricular standards that had not been a part of his program in the past, his self-esteem and self-confidence improved, and when asked about how he was doing by members of his IEP team, Brad said simply, "I feel awesome."

Personalization

"I have a caseload of 30 or more students. How can I get to know my students, especially when I am only the teacher of record and do not get to see all of them in every class?"

Personalization does not just happen. It takes purposeful planning and effort, and it must be viewed as a priority in transition planning for all students. Knowing the needs and backgrounds of students and being their advocate is the key to personalization. Teachers need to help students connect and have a sense of belonging in the school. Knowing the student helps teachers make the connections to his or her interests and to the people that are important to the student. It is not necessary that classroom teachers are always the primary advocate; there may be others who are more naturally connected to the student, such as a coach, a principal, a class sponsor, a peer, a sibling or an employer. The important thing is that the student has an advocate. It is important for adults to try to understand a student's style of dress, hairstyle, outside interests, family lifestyle and culture, extracurricular activities, technology interests, music, and so much more. This will build trust and understanding. Understanding aspects of personalization ties to person-centered approaches to transition planning.

> *Teachers need to help students connect and have a sense of belonging in the school. Knowing the student helps teachers make the connections to his or her interests and to the people that are important to the student.*

Person-centered planning has been discussed in special education literature for well over twenty years (O'Brien & O'Brien, 2000). It is a collaborative approach that expresses a set of inclusive values that centers on designing a student's life and supports through a range of tools and techniques (National Center on Secondary Education and Transition, 2003). The central premise is that any methods used must be reflective of the individual's personal communication mechanisms and assist him or her to outline needs, desires, and goals. There is no differentiation between the process used and the output and outcomes of the person-centered planning; instead it pursues social inclusion (e.g., community participation, employment) through inclusive means. Kendricks (2000) goes beyond the planning process and talks about person-centeredness. *Person-centeredness* is about intentionally being with people that may or may not include planning. It's about the relationship with others as described by his seven hallmarks:

- A commitment to know and seek to understand
- A conscious resolve to be of genuine service
- An openness to being guided by the person
- A willingness to struggle for difficult goals
- Flexibility, creativity, and openness to trying what might be possible
- A willingness to enhance the humanity and dignity of the person
- To look for the good in people and help to bring it out

Some of a student's interests and skills may lead to further education and career opportunities. Understanding the life struggles and challenges a student may help the advocate know what internal or external supports may be necessary to keep the student in school, graduate, and go on to meet his or her postsecondary goals.

 **Support for Carlos**

Carlos wants to attend college. However, he would be the first generation in his family to do so. His family is unfamiliar with how to navigate the maze of admission and financial aid requirements. In addition, Carlos is one of few Hispanic students in the school and sometimes feels disconnected. There are two adults who have helped Carlos find his place in high school. First, the assistant principal is also a first-generation college graduate. He got to know Carlos during freshman orientation and has kept tabs on him and has offered to help him work through the various applications. In addition, his English teacher got to know a bit about Carlo's background and culture through a writing assignment and the other activities that she did at the beginning of the semester. As she learned about Carlos's family, she encouraged him to talk about his culture with others in the class. She arranged for him to share some of the family traditions with her classes, and provided the support to ensure that he felt comfortable with this sharing.

Career Exploration

"How do I work on career activities when students are focused on trying to pass their classes?"

Career exploration can and should be embedded throughout the high school experience. All students should have an opportunity to explore their strengths, preferences and interests as they relate to possible future careers. Since most careers require varying levels of education (e.g., apprenticeships, program certificates/credentials, 2- or 4-year college), students need to understand the connection between the content they are learning, career possibilities and expectations, and necessary steps in between. Many career activities can be and should be embedded in the daily experiences of the classroom. For example, a teacher may use guest speakers, such as a meteorologist or environmental scientist, after each unit in the physical science class to talk to the class about their specific jobs and make connections between the unit's content and the career. Social studies classes might invite judges and other people involved in the government system to share information about their careers. In any content area, research projects can be used to explicitly explore careers. Finally, many electives provide skills directly tied to careers and other transition skills (e.g., work-study, personal finance, study skills class, career orientation class, adult roles and responsibilities class, child care).

Guidance counselors conduct a variety of career preparation activities throughout the high school years for all students. Many of these activities can serve as transition assessments and provide valuable information into the transition IEP and planning process. Special educators should ask their guidance counselors about some of the activities they conduct for all students, such as career interest inventories, graduation plans, college/career information, career counseling, college night where students can visit with a variety of colleges, job fairs of potential employers, and other valuable activities to ensure that students with disabilities have access to these resources and that the IEP team can take advantage of the information gleaned from them.

Transition planning meetings can provide an opportunity to review the planning and assessment work started by the guidance counselor, as well as a chance for students to see the connections between academic content and the careers in which the skills and content are applicable. For example, identifying a student's interests allows a teacher to talk with the student about content-area classes that link the knowledge from that class to potential careers. During a transition planning meeting, a teacher can engage the student in a conversation about the classes he or she likes and the specific content to support the student in thinking about a career. For example, a student enjoys his physical science class. The teacher could use this information to identify possible career interests and discuss with him the possible links to careers in geology, environmental sciences, and similar fields. This information could also help inform transition assessments and planning.

Many students have a difficult time seeing and understanding the "big picture" of schooling and how it ultimately relates and leads to future opportunities. Therefore it is important to help students connect success in required coursework to opportunities to gain admission into Career-Technical Center programs and postsecondary education. For example, having students visit the Career Tech or vocational education center in their freshman year provides a clear picture of what is offered and the requirements to participate, which may help a student set goals and develop a plan to reach the goal.

In addition to career-tech programs, many high schools offer a variety of opportunities to explore opportunities such as work-based learning, internships, mentorships, and project-based learning. Some high schools have moved to requiring senior projects, a capstone assignment that demonstrates their understanding of a topic of their choice. Senior projects blend traditional core and performance-based skills in a unique and rigorous exit program. Graduating seniors are required to demonstrate not only what they know but also what they are able to do. Some senior projects have a mentorship or internship component that affords students an opportunity to shadow in their intended area of study in college or for a career. By selecting a high-interest, relevant project topic, students can both learn from and enjoy the completion of this project. Information gained from this

Senior projects can help student identify and/or eliminate possible future careers. Students can identify preferences and aspects of the internship that met their strengths, desires, and needs. Information from the senior project should be included as part of the student's transition planning process.

A Teacher's View

My name is Brittany, and I have been teaching for over 15 years in a suburban high school in southern Indiana. Many of those years have been in a co-teaching environment. I have co-taught English and physical science. Currently I am co-teaching biology. When I co-taught English, we created and taught a career unit ([which] can be found in the appendix at the end of this chapter) that tied to some of the standards and was important in providing students insight into the future. Some may think that career units are only done in English; however, I believe, as do my co-teachers, that we need to infuse transition and career skills in all courses. In the physical science class, we always ended a unit with a guest speaker from the community who described their occupation and the necessary related skills.

From my experience, it is important to ensure that all students are provided transition planning. I was always amazed at how much students learned about themselves and the possibilities for careers that they had never considered.

and other similar type projects are provide one of the best embedded school activities for transition planning. Senior projects can help student identify and/or eliminate possible future careers. Students can identify preferences and aspects of the internship that met their strengths, desires, and needs. Information from the senior project should be included as part of the student's transition planning process.

 ## The Start of Myisha's Nursing Career

In their first year of high school, all three of our students were able to visit the career center and see the wide range of programs and pathways that would be available to them. They also learned of the educational requirements needed to be admitted and complete the career center. During this visit, Myisha became interested in a career in nursing. Because the high school has a senior project requirement, she began to consider what topic in the field of nursing she would explore. With the support of her teacher of record and guidance counselor, Myisha obtained a job-shadowing experience in the pediatric department of the local hospital. Here they helped her identify the areas she will have to demonstrate her self-advocacy skills and coping strategies as identified in her transition IEP.

When it came time to submit her senior project proposal, Myisha focused on pediatric nursing and chose the topic of childhood diabetes for her research. She was able to intern at the children's clinic at the local hospital. This culminating experience was included in her portfolio and helped her gain admission to nursing school.

Inclusive Program Practices

How do I find time to support my students in an inclusive classroom and still conduct transition assessments for all my students?

The simple answer to this question is to broaden the sources of information and environments where the information is gathered so that the process becomes a collaborative effort. This will require a structure for communication, an understanding of roles and responsibilities, and an awareness of the various activities already being offered in the school or that should be offered.

Communication Structures

Communication structures can be developed to allow consistent and regular communication between special education personnel and others involved with the student. This includes situations where the student's teacher of record is different from the teacher of service. Establishing collaborative communication structures should start at the beginning of the year so that teachers have an understanding of the information that is being requested, as well as its purpose and use. For example, the special educator would either meet or share electronically with the general education teacher the types of information/data (e.g., accommodations, learning strategies, areas of interests, organizational skills) that support transition annual goals for the students on their caseload.

Co-teaching

In a truly inclusive environment, many transition activities will be provided to all students. Co-teaching is one way to support greater inclusion for students and ensure access, and it is also a natural way to communicate and gather information. By being involved in inclusive classrooms, the special educator is gathering information for the transition assessments as a part of that co-teaching role. Teachers in a co-teaching setting also have a greater opportunity to make sure that transition activities are implemented within the classroom for all students. In addition, unique activities for certain students may be provided within the general education classroom or in a study skills/resource environment.

 **Benefits of Co-teaching**

Brad and Myisha are in a co-taught history class. Their teacher of record is not the special education teacher in the class. Therefore, the teacher of record spoke with both of the teachers (general educator and special educator) to inform them of the kinds of information she needs for both Brad and Myisha. The history teacher shared with her the various units for the semester. They agree that progress would be monitored on line and that the history teacher would support Brad and Myisha with compiling evidence for their portfolios. In addition, the special education co-teacher would gather data for their transition IEP annual goals.

Student Portfolios

Student portfolios are a strategy for gathering evidence from inclusive classrooms. A portfolio is a collection of work that demonstrates a student's acquisition of knowledge, skills, and attitudes. It gives a picture of a student's experience in a learning situation. The process of selecting portfolio content and/or presenting the portfolio should promote reflective thinking and encourage a student to be self-directed in determining future learning or career. It is an excellent opportunity to demonstrate both growth in the acquisition of the knowledge, skills, and attitudes and level of competency in certain academic, social/emotional, and career areas.

Student portfolios give responsibility and ownership to the student, an excellent self-determination or transition skill to be taught. Portfolios can provide evidence of the transition assessments used throughout a student's high school years and as part of the transition IEP. It provides an orderly sequence of the activities that have occurred and can easily be referenced. Items that might make up the portfolio include

- Student self-evaluation reflection forms
- Interest inventories
- Writing samples
- Log of career exploration activities
- Learning-style inventories
- Other transition assessments

School Support Personnel

Guidance counselors also play an important role in helping all students transition from high school to adulthood. In a truly inclusive high school, all counselors have students with disabilities as part of their caseload. Counselors are vital to helping students create graduation plans, and explore possible colleges and careers, and they provide resources to help students have a better understanding of various careers. They also play an important role in helping to identify the additional supports, both internal and external, that a student may need. Finally, it is often the guidance counselor who knows the unique life struggles that a student may be having. Similarly, school psychologist and social workers play an important role in supporting students.

There are some other excellent transition activities that have historically been reserved for students with IEPs. Many of these could be expanded and offered to all students. Many high schools already offer college and career fairs. Integrating the unique information for students with disabilities should be a part of these fairs, such as what support and service agencies have to offer and instruction about rights and responsibilities. Meeting with students to help them think about their future and creating a written plan on how to get there are good for all students. Just as students with disabilities may create transition portfolios, creating a portfolio of high school activities is applicable for many students. Some high schools have already established student portfolios as a general requirement. In many ways, the knowledge base in the special education field has created and developed a good process that should be used with many, if not all students.

Table 4.2 provides a list of guiding questions for teachers to use to be purposeful and deliberate in identifying transition skills and activities in the general education settings. As students move through high school, the foundational components and universal transition services described previously continue to support student growth and learning as students move toward graduation.

INTERNAL AND EXTERNAL SUPPORTS

There are some students who will need additional services and supports to be successful in high school and beyond. In the conceptual framework, we depict these supports as internal and external supports that can be accessed by any student; however, some are unique for students with disabilities. As stated in Chapter 1, it is important to be aware

Table. 4.2. Guiding questions for teachers to identify transition skills and activities in general education settings

Guiding Questions for Teachers to Identify Transition Skills and Activities
• What is the general education teacher teaching this semester? What are the units and activities?
• What pre-assessments are teachers using to determine the appropriate levels of instruction?
• What activities do teachers use to get to know their students?
• Do teachers use any cooperative learning activities?
• Is the student receiving the necessary supports to be successful in an inclusive environment? If not, what are alternative solutions?
• What tools do teachers use/teach to develop organizational and study skills?
• Who is the student's school advocate?
• What are the communication structures that will facilitate collaboration and coordination?
• What activities are offered in the school for career exploration?
• What are the activities provided by the guidance department that connect to transition activities?

Possible Transition Skills and Activities That May Be Found in the General Education Settings	
• Choice-making	• Leadership/empowerment
• Cooking	• Learning strategies
• Employability and careers	• Life skills
• Goal-setting	• Money management/finance
• Health and wellness	• Problem solving
• Home maintenance	• Safety
• Self-determination	• Self-advocacy
• Social and communication	• Self-awareness
• Teamwork	• Transportation/mobility

that these internal and external supports are identified and used to supplement high school and transition services, not supplant.

Internal supports are the services that are provided by school districts or special education planning units. Examples of these have been described throughout this chapter, such as accommodations and modifications, other special education services, social work services, guidance counselors, career counseling, service learning, suicide prevention or antibullying programs, and so forth. External supports are community resources provided through collaborative relationships and can be necessary to ensure graduation and postsecondary success. Examples include vocational rehabilitation counseling, transportation services, or even businesses providing internships. Some external support resources are challenging for teachers, students, and families to connect with due to the different eligibility criteria, documentation needs, and funding requirements. Therefore it is imperative that teachers understand the wide range of services offered, whom to contact for information, and how to connect students and families to these resources and supports. Both internal and external supports are based on the needs of the students. Table 4.3 provides examples of internal and external supports.

SUMMARY

Schools are charged with preparing all students, with and without disabilities, to be contributing members of their community. Some students leave high school and enter the workforce; other students pursue additional education prior to starting their careers. Regardless of their path, the outcomes for success are dependent on quality instruction, academic rigor and standards, personalization, career exploration, and inclusive practices. When planning for students with disabilities, it is critical to consider all of the elements in the framework in the context of individual planning. This chapter has shown ways to include transition planning as an integral and unified process that uses the general education environment and promotes positive postschool outcomes for all, with considerations for all students, including those who need additional internal and external supports. The

Table 4.3. Internal and external support examples

Internal Supports	External Supports
Adaptations and accommodations	Business partnerships
Antibullying program	Developmental disabilities services
Assistive technology	Family support services
Behavior consultant	Foster care
Curricular modifications	Health services
Occupational therapy services	Mental health services
Peer supports	One-stop career centers
Physical therapy services	Postsecondary education disability support services
Service learning	Substance abuse and addiction services
Social worker supports	Social services (e.g., housing, food stamps)
Special education services	Transportation services
Speech-language pathology services	Juvenile justice system
School psychology services	Vocational rehabilitation
School counseling programs and services	
School nursing services	
Suicide-prevention program	

appendixes that follow include blank versions of forms used in some activities described in this chapter, as well as sample unit plans that illustrate how transition skills can be found across content areas. The next chapter will address approaches for working with students with more significant support needs.

FOR FURTHER INFORMATION

Differentiating Instruction

Tomlinson, C.A., & Eidson, C.C. (2003). *Differentiation in practice: A resource guide for differentiating curriculum.* Alexandria, VA: Association for Supervision and Curriculum Development.

Guide to planning and teaching process for making curriculum responsive to all learners

Tomlinson, C.A., Brimijoin, K. & Narvaez, L. (2008). *The differentiated school: Making revolutionary changes in teaching and learning.* Alexandria, VA: Association for Supervision and Curriculum Development.

Examples and overarching strategy for implementing differentiated instruction schoolwide

Thomas, C.A., Bartholomew, C.C., & Scott, L.A. (2009). *Universal design for transition: A roadmap for planning and instruction.* Baltimore: Paul H. Brookes Publishing Co.

Addresses how universal design for learning can be used to reach all students when teaching related to transition

Activities and Assessments Utilizing Multiple Intelligences and Learning Styles to Better Understand Your Students

What's Your Learning Style?
http://www.edutopia.org/multiple-intelligences-learning-styles-quiz
A 24-question learning-style assessment

Assessment: Find Your Strengths!
http://www.literacyworks.org/mi/assessment/findyourstrengths.html
A questionnaire that helps determine which areas of intelligence are a person's greatest strengths.

Learning Styles
http://www.ldpride.net/learningstyles.MI.htm
Information and tests on learning style preferences

C.I.T.E. Learning Styles Instrument
http://wvabe.org/CITE/cite.pdf
Brief assessment and tips for different learning styles

Cooperative Learning Rubrics

Middle and high school collaboration rubric
http://www2.uwstout.edu/content/profdev/rubrics/secondaryteamworkrubric.html
Rubric for student use in evaluating themselves and/or their peers

Cooperative Learning Rubric
http://www.readwritethink.org/files/resources/lesson_images/lesson95/coop_rubric.pdf
General rubric for students to self-assess or evaluate their peers

Person-Centered Planning

Cornell University's Person Centered Planning Education Site

http://www.ilr.cornell.edu/edi/pcp/course07.html

A brief online course about person-centered planning for transition

Inclusive Solutions

http://www.inclusive-solutions.com/pcplanning.asp

Examples and illustrations of person-centered planning strategies

Pacer Center

http://www.pacer.org/tatra/resources/personal.asp

Overview of person-centered planning with links to additional resources

Senior Project

http://www.seniorproject.net/

Official site with guidelines and resources for capstone projects

Co-teaching

Chapman, C., & Hart-Hyatt, C. (2011). *Critical conversations in co-teaching: A problem solving approach.* Bloomington, IN: Solution Tree.

Focuses on the communication needed for effective collaborative teaching

Gregory, G.H. (2011). *Differentiated instruction.* Thousand Oaks, CA: Corwin.

Compilation of practical strategies for effectively differentiating instruction

Coil, (2007). *Successful teaching in the differentiated classroom.* Marion, IL: Pieces of Learning.

Strategies and examples for how to differentiate instruction

Potts, E.A., & Howard, L.A. (2011). *How to co-teach: A guide for general and special educators.* Baltimore, MD: Paul H. Brookes Publishing Co.

Addresses both educators' perspectives and advises on how to maximize the benefits of a co-teaching partnership

Strickland, C.A. (2007). *Tools for high-quality differentiated instruction.* Alexandria, VA: ASCD.

Binder containing practical material and examples illustrating how to use it

Student Portfolios

Portfolio Assessment

http://www.pgcps.org/~elc/portfolio.html

General information about using portfolios as a method of assessment

Nevada Transition Portfolio

http://transitioncoalition.org/transition/section.php?pageId=163

Describes example of one state's portfolio program

Special Education Transition Portfolio

http://www.rockingham.k12.va.us/rcps_sped/svrp/Transition-Portfolio.htm

A checklist and set of documents to compile beginning in 7th grade

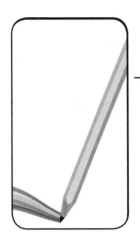

Appendix A

Examples of Content Area Units

U.S. History: Grade 11

Integrated Math and Consumer Science: Grade 9

Health and Wellness: Grades 8 & 9

Science: Grades 9 & 10

Spanish: Grade 10

English (Career Unit): Grade 11

U.S. History

Unit Description: Students are introduced to a unit of study that examines American history through the lens of civil rights and promotes civic participation. Students are introduced to key periods of four social movements that have had great impact on the nation's history: the women's suffrage movement, the children's rights movement, the African American civil rights movement), the disability rights movements. Over the course of study, students choose one movement to research, investigating the associated injustices, strategies, and achievements. After demonstrating their understanding of the past in the form of a case study, students apply what they have learned to current-day civil rights issues, raising public awareness and promoting action.

Grade Level: 11   **Content Area(s): U.S. History**

Step 1: Desired Results/Outcomes

Standards/Established Goals

USH.1.3 Describe controversies pertaining to slavery, abolitionism, *Dred Scott v. Sanford* and social reform movements. (Government, Economics)

USH.3.6 Identify the contributions to American culture made by individuals and groups. (Individuals, Society, and Culture)

USH.3.8 Describe the Progressive movement and its impact on political, economic and social reform. (Government; Economics; Individuals, Society, and Culture)

USH.6.2 Summarize the early struggle for civil rights and identify events and people associated with this struggle. (Government; Economics; Individuals, Society, and Culture).

USH.6.3 Describe the constitutional significance and lasting effects of the United States Supreme Court case *Brown v. Board of Education*. (Government; Economics; Individuals, Society, and Culture)

USH.7.1 Explain the civil rights movement of the 1960s and 1970s by describing the ideas and actions of federal and state leaders, grassroots movements, and central organizations that were active in the movement. (Government; Economics; Individuals, Society, and Culture)

USH.7.2 Read Reverend Martin Luther King, Jr.'s "I Have a Dream" speech (1963) and "Letter from Birmingham Jail" (1963) and summarize the main ideas in each. (Government, Economics)

USH.9.2 Locate and analyze primary sources and secondary sources related to an event or issue of the past.

USH.9.5 Use technology in the process of conducting historical research and in the presentation of the products of historical research and current events.

11-12.RH.1 Cite specific textual evidence to support analysis of primary and secondary sources, connecting insights gained from specific details to an understanding of the text as a whole.

11-12.RH.2 Determine the central ideas or information of a primary or secondary source; provide an accurate summary that makes clear the relationships among the key details and ideas.

11-12.RH.3 Evaluate various explanations for actions or events and determine which explanation best accords with textual evidence, acknowledging where the text leaves matters uncertain.

Global Understandings:	**Essential Question(s):**
• We all have a role in shaping our rights. • Social justice begins with individuals. • Social movements rely on similar principles/values/methods. • Rights are not static; they can change over time. • History is written with a point of view. • The definition of equality expanded throughout U.S. history. • Research is not only found in books.	• Why is it important to have multiple perspectives in our democracy? • How can the ordinary citizen influence democracy? • What are civil rights and how are they earned? • What is the relationship between civil rights and democracy? • What is equality? How has the concept of equality changed and expanded in our history? • Whose history?

(continued)

What students will KNOW:	What students will BE ABLE TO DO:
• Specific legal and illegal methods for fighting injustice • Amendments to the Constitution and other laws that changed people's rights • The aspects of the Constitution and its interpretation that limited people's rights • Key court cases that supported injustices and key cases that overturned those injustices • The outcomes of four social movements • Definitions of equality, democracy, civil rights, social movements • Examples of legal, social, and economic forms of injustice • Important civil rights leaders • Important people and organizations that address social causes today • Timeline of the expansion of civil rights in American history	• Find appropriate research sources, including primary sources, on the Internet and using research databases • Analyze primary and secondary sources such as maps, graphs, charts, newspapers, diaries, timelines, political cartoons, surveys, media, interviews, and music • Recognize bias and multiple points of view in historical sources • Write a case study about a specific civil rights movement that analyzes the causes of social change and the methods used to achieve results • Identify a civil rights issue of today that meets the criteria they developed for a social movement • Create citations • Identify a current civil rights issue and conduct research to find solutions • Work with a group to create and deliver a multimedia and oral presentation • Take action on their recommendations from that campaign

Step 2: Planning for Academic Diversity

LEARNING BARRIER	POSSIBLE SOLUTIONS	WEB RESOURCES
Limited knowledge on citation of sources	Use both electronic and hard copy examples	http://www.citationmachine.net/index2.php
Struggles with information gathering	Primary and secondary sources available in classroom and online, graphic organizer, folders	http://news.google.com/
Content specific information	Provide multiple media outlets for civil rights information	http://www.civilrights.org/
Information on organizing reform movements	Provide multiple media sources for reform efforts, reenactments	http://www.acorn.org/index.php?id=2716
Struggles with comprehension	Wikipedia, multiple text sources, read out loud	www.wikipedia.com www.readoutloud.com

(continued)

Step 3: Assessment Evidence

Summative Assessment/Performance Task

Create a campaign around a civil rights issue of today from the following list or something of your own choosing that has been approved by the teacher.

- Environmental rights
- Protection from racial profiling
- Educational rights
- Privacy rights

The criteria for your campaign are the following:

Describe a current civil rights issue.

- What the issue is about?
- What is the purpose of the campaign?
- What are the reasons why the campaign is important?

Connect to a past civil rights movement.

- A past injustice or method of resistance
- Who, where, and when the incident took place
- How one primary source shows evidence of the injustice or method

* Relates the past injustice or method to the current civil rights issue

* Connects the past to the current movement's goals

Use information about the issue from two articles.

- Use reliable sources
- Explain an important aspect of the issue

Clearly and accurately describe two organizations involved in the issue that

- Support civil rights for the group
- Provide fair and accurate information

Select an appropriate nonviolent method of action (march, boycott, strike, sit-in, protest, demonstration, vote).

- Includes an example or link to the method.
- The method helps people create awareness of the issue or send a message to an elected representative.

Preassessment

Four-square activity on current understanding of civil rights

Formative/Ongoing Assessments

Define civil rights.

- Analyze photographs and decide which rights are being violated.
- Read the movement profiles and write responses.
- Analyze legal achievements of civil rights movements.
- Choose a civil rights movement to study.

Understand injustice.

- Read the movement background.
- Define political, social, and economic rights.
- Take notes on the movement timeline.
- Analyze five primary sources.

Study methods of action.

- Re-enact a historical nonviolent protest.
- Continue taking notes on the movement timeline.
- Analyze five primary sources.
- Find information about civil rights leaders on the Library of Congress web site.

Describe a movement.

- Sort your research notes and identify the focus of your case study.
- Complete the graphic organizer.
- Write the first draft of your case study.
- Write the final draft of your case study.
- Get together with a group and share your case study.

(continued)

Use correct grammar and spelling. • No major grammatical errors • No major spelling errors You may use the following website to help with your research: http://rights.teachingmatters.org/step5	
Possible Focused Transition Skills • Empowerment • Self-determination skills • Self-advocacy • Self-awareness • Collaboration/team skills • Rights and responsibilities	

Consumer Science and Integrated Math

Unit Description: Buying a Car

Grade Level: 9th	**Content Area(s): Consumer Science and Integrated Math I**

Step 1: Desired Results/Outcomes

Standards/Established Goals

Consumer Science "Personal Financial Responsibility" Standards:

PFR-1.4 Make financial decisions by systematically considering alternatives and consequences.

PFR-3.4.1 Evaluate impact of external factors (such as marketing, advertising and the economy) on spending decisions.

PFR-3.4.2 Justify consumer buying decisions by evaluating external factors.

PFR-3.4.3 Evaluate opportunity costs (such as owning versus renting a house, purchasing or leasing an auto).

Common Core Literacy for Technical Subjects Standards: (Under "Integration of Knowledge and Ideas")

9-10.RT.7 Translate technical information expressed in words in a text into visual form (e.g., a table or chart) and translate information expressed visually or mathematically (e.g., in an equation) into words.

9-10.WT.8 Gather relevant information from multiple authoritative print and digital sources, using advanced searches effectively; assess the usefulness of each source in answering the research question.

Common Core State Standards Integrated Math I:

Relationships between quantities

- Reason quantitatively and use units to solve problems
- Interpret the structure of expressions
- Create equations that describe numbers or relationships

Descriptive statistics

- Summarize, represent, and interpret data on a single-count or measurement variable
- Summarize, represent, and interpret data on two categorical and quantitative variables

Global Understandings:	**Essential Question(s):**
- Making good consumer decisions requires information gathering and thoughtful consideration of preferences, needs, and resources. - Mathematics is useful for making good consumer decisions and life choices. - Technology, used well, informs good consumer decisions and life choices.	- If I decide I need a car, how do I know which one to choose? - How can I use my math skills to evaluate the car I'd like to buy? - How can I use technology to evaluate the car I'd like to buy?

(continued)

What students will KNOW:	What students will BE ABLE TO DO:
• Expenses related to car purchase: purchase price, taxes, fees • Expenses related to car ownership: license fees, registration, insurance • Expenses related to car operation: gas, oil changes, maintenance, scheduled repairs, unscheduled repairs, miles per gallon • Consumer information sources • Reliable online sources	• Identify online sources that provide accurate, updated information • Use online consumer information sources to compare and contrast products • Calculate the cost of owning particular vehicles

Step 2: Planning for Academic Diversity

LEARNING BARRIER	POSSIBLE SOLUTIONS	WEB RESOURCES
No access to technology at home	Provide increased opportunity to access technology of school's resources for students with no tech resources at home	
Difficulty with reading	Pair/group students with varying reading levels Provide reading material at varied levels of sophistication Provide charts/graphs with necessary information Read passages out loud	wikispaces.org
Difficulty with identifying and following multiple-step procedures	Provide structured and scaffolded steps with hints about where to find specific types of information	
Difficulty interpreting technical data	Provide individualized or small-group direct support	
Difficulty with speaking and/or reading in English	Seek and provide some translations in native language when available Partner with bilingual classmate when available	wikispaces.org

Possible Focused Transition Skills:

• Budgeting and money management

• Problem solving

• Learning community resources

• Comparison shopping

• Technology skills

Health and Wellness

Unit Description: "You Are What You Eat" (Adapted from Tomlinson & McTighe, 2006)

Grade Level: 8/9th	Duration: 3 weeks	Content Area(s): Health and Wellness

Step 1: Desired Results/Outcomes

Standards/Established Goals

Academic standards for Health & Wellness, Grade 8 or 9

For this unit, the following standards will be focused particularly on food and nutrition and can be easily adapted for older or younger students.

— Analyze the relationship between healthy behaviors and personal health.

— Examine how the family influences the health of adolescents.

— Describe the influence of culture on health beliefs, practices and behaviors.

— Access valid health information from home, school and community.

— Apply effective verbal and nonverbal communication skills to enhance health.

— Distinguish between healthy and unhealthy alternatives to health-related issues or problems.

— State a health-enhancing position on a topic and support it with accurate information; demonstrate how to influence and support others to make positive health choices

Global Understandings:	**Essential Question(s):**
• A balanced diet contributes to physical and mental health.	• What is healthy eating?
• Poor nutrition leads to a variety of health problems.	• Am I a healthy eater?
• Healthful eating requires one to act on available information about good nutrition, even if it means breaking comfortable habits.	• How do I decide what to eat?
	• Could a healthy diet for one person be unhealthy for another?
	• What health problems could thin people have?
• The USDA provides guidelines and recommendations for nutrition that vary according to personal characteristics.	• Given all the available information on good nutrition, why do so many people have health problems caused by poor nutrition?

What students will KNOW:	**What students will BE ABLE TO DO:**
• Key nutrition terms (*protein, fat, calorie, carbohydrate, cholesterol,* etc.)	• Read and interpret nutrition information on food labels
• Types of food and their nutritional values	• Analyze diets for nutritional value
• USDA food categories and guidelines	• Plan balanced diets for themselves and others
• Variables influencing nutritional needs	• Develop a personal action plan for healthy eating
• Specific health problems caused by poor nutrition (e.g., diabetes, heart disease)	• Communicate information about good nutrition for a particular audience using writing and images

Source: Tomlinson and McTighe (2006).

(continued)

Step 2: Planning for Academic Diversity		
LEARNING BARRIER	**POSSIBLE SOLUTIONS**	**WEB RESOURCES**
Lack of resources	Direct students to particular resources	http://www.life123.com/health/nutrition/index.shtml http://www.choosemyplate.gov/guidelines/index.html http://myplate.com
Access to technology	Allow students with little access at home to have more time with classroom computer Print some of the info for students lacking access	
Teasing or bullying surrounding weight issues	Address concerns directly and sensitively	http://www.bodypositive.com/childwt.htm (resource for teacher)
Reading comprehension	Find sources with simplified language or use technology to read out loud to students	http://readoutloud.com/ http://simple.wikipedia.org/wiki/Main_Page
Difficulty organizing information	Use graphic organizer	http://freeology.com/graphicorgs/
Writing or editing difficulties	Peer editing Online editing	http://ghotit.com/dyslexia-online-spell-check

Summative Assessment/Performance Task

Chow Down: Students develop a three-day menu for meals and snacks for an upcoming outdoor education camp experience. They write a letter to the camp director to explain why their menu should be selected based on nutrition and taste.

Personal Eating Action Plan: Students prepare a plan for healthy eating based on their own unique characteristics (e.g., height, weight, activity level, special dietary needs, etc.). The plan will include nutrition goals and action plans needed to achieve those goals.

Preassessment

Writing Prompt: Describe two health problems that could arise as a result of poor nutrition and explain what changes in eating could help to avoid them.

Observations: Observe student eating habits during lunch.

Eating Diaries: Ask students to keep track of their eating for 24 hours and then rate the nutritional quality of their eating during that time period on a scale of 1–10.

Quiz: Ungraded true or false questions regarding nutrition facts and myths.

Formative/Ongoing Assessments

Family Meals: Students work in groups to evaluate eating habits of a hypothetical family whose diet is not healthy. They make recommendations for a diet that will improve nutritional value of meals.

(continued)

	Nutritional Brochure: Students create an illustrated brochure to teach younger children about the importance of good nutrition and the problems associated with poor eating. **Quiz**: On USDA nutrition guidelines **Quiz**: On nutrition terms
Possible Focused Transition Skills: • Healthy lifestyle and wellness • Choice-making skills • Self-awareness • Community health care resources	

Science

Unit Overview: Ecosystems (science) and text analysis (language arts)

Grade level: 9, 10   Length of Unit: Two weeks

Step 1: Desired Results/Outcomes

Established Goals/Standards

9-10 R.S. 9 Literacy Standard: Analyze how two or more texts address similar themes or topics in order to build knowledge or to compare the approaches the authors take.

Common Core Standard: Describe the relationship between living and nonliving components of ecosystems and describe how that relationship is in flux due to natural changes and human actions.

Global Understanding(s):	Essential Question(s):
• I am a part of an ecosystem(s), and my decisions impact the ecosystem(s). • The amount of life environments can support is limited by available resources. • Human activities and natural phenomena impact ecosystems. • The interaction among climate and birth and death of organism contribute to the long-term stability of an ecosystem. • Similarly themed texts contain both validating and dissenting information/opinions.	• What elements and relationships make up an ecosystem? • How do my decisions and actions support and undo my ecosystem? • To what extent might my analysis on similarly themed text help me define/defend my point of view?
What Students will KNOW:	**What students will BE ABLE TO DO:**
• Complex relationships • Observing habitats • Text analysis • Themes • Life environments • Elements • Available resources • Ecosystems • Relationships • Driving forces • Pressures of the environment • State of the environment • Impacts • Responses of policy and regulation	• Compare complex ecological relationships, with regard to available resources, human activities, and natural phenomena • Categorize environments as living and nonliving • Identify, analyze and compare themes across texts • Identify varied habitats within ecosystems • Describe living and nonliving relationships within ecosystems • Use graphic organizer appropriate to the analysis

(continued)

Step 2: Planning for Academic Diversity		
LEARNING BARRIER	**POSSIBLE SOLUTIONS**	**WEB RESOURCES**
Text comprehension	Audio versions of the text Same content, less complicated text	Read out loud Wiki—simple English
Low vision	Audio version Large print	
Limited attention span	Chunked text Brief discussions, draw symbols or take notes to capture key ideas	

Step 3: Assessment Evidence

Summative Assessment/Performance Task

As a member of a renowned international team, you have identified an urban ecosystem that is within two miles of your home. You have studied the works of experts in the field and have identified several potential human and natural forces that are impacting the ecosystems.

In preparing your report for the funder of your project, you will need to include:

- A vivid description (written/drawn/map) of the ecosystem, including . . .
- A diagram of the ecosystem
- A review of the literature describing the negative impacts on the ecosystem
- A discussion of ways in which either the natural forces or the human impact might be mitigated to reduce impact on the ecosystem

Your funder has asked your presentation to take one of the following forms:

- Crisp, easy-to-follow PowerPoint presentation
- Colorful, well-written, tri-fold brochure
- Box diagram
- Photo album

Other Evidence

Preassessment—four-square about what they already know about the square.

Frayer model: What is an ecosystem?

Formative/Ongoing assessments

Double-entry journal

Quiz on vocabulary

Discussions

Participation

Reflection

Types of assessment

- Whole-group discussion: purposes of assessment
- A comparison document between the texts and meaning of ecosystem.
- Students will create a product (i.e., essay, T chart, Venn diagram) to compare the books.
- Students will create a diagram of an ecosystem within two miles of their house.

Postassessment:

- Self-reflection: Look at someone else's ecosystem diagram.
- Decide what you would think differently about yours and what suggestions might you make about theirs, based on the rubric.

Step 4: Learning Plan	
Introduction of Unit:	
Short read: Newspaper or web site article on destruction of ecosystem Complete a four-square with the essential questions as a preassessment of student knowledge Complex relationships	
Sequential List of Learning Activities **Day 1:** Reading: George, J.C. (1971). *Who Really Killed Cock Robin?* New York, NY: Harper Trophy. Seuss, T. (1971). *The Lorax*. New York, NY: Random House. • Using a Venn diagram, T-chart, or compare-and-contrast statements, students will compare the two texts for similarities and differences in their discussion of ecosystems. **Day 2:** Using the Classification of Urban ecosystems diagram students will apply the text Lorax or Cock Robin to classify ecosystem elements based on classification of driving forces, pressures of environment, state of the environment, impacts of pollution, and responses on various policy information. • Using the human ecosystems diagram students will develop a framework for the impact of human ecosystems. • In order to examine the ecosystem around the school, students will take field measurements of the school ecosystems and apply the knowledge of field measurements to their home ecosystem. • Topics for active discussion • What should be recycled, what should be put back into the ground? • What did you do yesterday that supported or damaged the system that you live in? **Assessment:** Types of Assessment • Whole-group discussion: purposes of assessment • A comparison document between the texts and meaning of ecosystem • Students will create a product (i.e., essay, T-chart, Venn diagram) to compare the books. • Students will create a diagram of an ecosystem within two miles of their house. The diagram includes habitats, relationships, and categorizes environments as living and nonliving.	Differentiated by readiness to support kids' levels of deeper understanding by the teacher working with one group to support their text analysis of complex relationships, living and nonliving, life environments and habitats. Individually or small group, can complete the classification on chart paper of lined paper. **Anchor Activities:** Two different views of global warming on the world as a whole What are the differences between urban, suburban, and rural ecosystems?

(continued)

Paper Toss	
• What skills did you take away from this unit?	
• How will you live differently within your ecosystem?	
Possible Focused Transition Skills:	
• Leadership skills	
• Community living skills	
• Community responsibility	

Spanish

Spanish II[a]

Step 1 – Desired Results/Outcomes

Established Goals/Standards

10.1.1 Use multiple greetings and farewells in various situations.

10.1.2 Accurately state basic information about self and others.

10.1.4 Exchange familiar information and opinions in brief conversations.

10.1.5 Exchange familiar information and opinions in written form.

10.1.6 Make requests and ask different types of questions.

10.1.8 Use speaking and listening strategies to facilitate communication.

10.3.1 Present prepared material on a variety of topics.

10.3.2 Read passages aloud to demonstrate improving intonation and pronunciation.

10.3.3 Compose simple cohesive written information using appropriate formats with teacher guidance.

10.3.4 Describe objects, self, and others in written and spoken language with greater detail.

Global Understanding(s):	**Essential Question(s):**
• Communication is important.	• How do we provide information to people?
• Information can be communicated to people in several different ways.	• What is effective communication?
• Shared meaning is critical in written and verbal communication.	• How do you engage someone in conversation?

What Students will KNOW:	**What students will BE ABLE TO DO:**
Greetings, farewells, sentence structure, correct pronunciation	Translate greetings, farewells, and basic English into Spanish
Elements of scripted dialogue	Construct a basic self-descriptive interview protocol
Interview protocol	Communicate basic greetings, farewells, and self-information using written and oral Spanish
Speaking and listening strategies	
Self-descriptive vocabulary terms, questioning strategies	

Step 2: Planning for Academic Diversity		
LEARNING BARRIER	**POSSIBLE SOLUTIONS**	**RESOURCES**
Written literacy in Spanish	Scaffolding sentence structure and written communication	Textbook and children's books in Spanish Translation software: www.babblefish.com/free translator.php Peers
Verbal literacy in Spanish	Scaffolding spoken language	Recorded statements Peer practice

(continued)

Weak comprehension of native language grammar rules	Reteach of native language grammar rules	Grammar rules book
		Minilessons on grammar
Limited communication skills in native language	Practice and scaffolding in native language	Part of speech resources: Books, flash cards
Student with hearing impairments		Audio recordings
		Written resources

Possible resources:

Step 3: Assessment Evidence

Summative Assessment/Performance Task

Do you remember how you felt as a first year Spanish student? So, as a second-year Spanish student, you and a partner have been asked to demonstrate your current skills through video-taped interviews to share with the new first-year students. You will be showing your ability to write and speak, in Spanish, greetings, farewells, and basic information about yourself. You will write up the interview questions in Spanish and, with your partner, videotape yourselves interviewing each other.

The interview should begin with basic greetings and end with proper farewells. The interview should consist of a minimum of eight questions, and each person should write her/his own questions. Questions should be given to your interviewee (partner) at least two days in advance of the videotaping so that she/he can prepare answers.

For More Advanced students:

You have been selected by the school district administration to create welcome resources and school information to native Spanish speakers. First you must interview a native Spanish speaker to determine what information would be most pertinent to them if being welcomed to a school. As a result of the interview you will complete one of the following tasks:

• Creating a welcome video

• Developing welcome letter for parent and student

• Creating a questionnaire for relevant information the school needs to know

• Translating current school signs and information into Spanish

Other Evidence

Preassessment

Students will play a concentration/matching game with English and Spanish greetings, farewells, and basic self-descriptive terms.

Students will be asked to write three basic terms that describe themselves, in Spanish, as an exit card.

Advanced Students:

• Students will translate page 5 of the current student handbook.

• Students will read their translated page 5 with the teacher.

Formative/Ongoing assessments

• Discussions/shared understandings

• Review of interview questions and responses

• Oral communication

• Written communication via practice questions and terminology

• Listening and responding

• Quiz

Step 4: Learning Plan
Sequential List of Learning Activities
• Discuss interview protocol creation, develop good questions, discuss effective interviewing skills
• Review greetings and farewell and discuss different ways to greet individuals and engage them in conversation
• Practice interview protocol with peers
• Share outcomes of the interview
• Establish student groupings or working alone; students choose which task they will work on.
• Shared examples: review/discuss/question
• Establish goals and timelines for each subtask to be completed
Possible Focused Transition Skills:
• Community skills
• Learning about self and others
• Self-determination

[a]The authors drew upon the Indiana state standards for the creation of this content area unit.

English

English 11—Career Unit

This unit is designed to help you analyze and prepare for life after high school. You must turn in each of the assignments together in a packet. Each will be awarded points separately. To be successful in this unit, you need to follow directions exactly.

Appearance and quality count: All work must be typewritten, proofread, and spell checked. Accuracy of mechanics, grammar, spelling, punctuation, and usage will count toward grades. You may present this information in paragraph or bullet form.

Assignment #1: Career Exploration

Identify THREE potential jobs/careers you are interested in pursuing. Complete ALL of the following information for each job/career you list. Each bullet below is required for each job/career:

- State the job/career path you seek. Be specific.
- Explain why you are interested in the career you have selected as a potential job/career, going beyond superficial reasons. Be specific. What attracts you to this job?
- Explain why you have chosen your intended job/career. What interests you about this career and why? Be specific. You may do this separately or make a comparison/contrast chart if you wish.
- Identify which of the three colleges is your number one college choice based upon your analysis of these three colleges. Write a brief statement identifying your first choice and explaining why you have selected it as such.

Assignment #2: Your Job Outlook

Provide a statement that analyzes the short- and long-term job outlook for your intended job. The best source for gathering the following information is the Occupational Informational Network that can be found at http://www.onetonline.org/.

Consider and include the following required information. Be sure to answer all parts of each question.

A. What are the short- and the long-term job outlooks for this career field? Is this a career field that is currently in demand? What is the long-range forecast for this career? Is it a growing or a declining field?

Support your statements with statistics from career databases.

Use the databases and other resources to answer the following information:

Minimum educational requirements:

- Does this career/job require technical training, certification, or licensure?
- State the required training for initial employment.
- Identify a college or training program in- or out-of-state for each career/job that requires it. [Note: This may include trade schools, vocational schools, community colleges, four-year colleges, apprenticeships, etc.]
- What are the admission criteria for this training? Do you meet the criteria? Create a list of the minimum admission criteria, and check off all the criteria that you meet?
- How much will the training cost? How will you pay for it?

B. Is this field changing in any ways? What additional skills will be necessary in the future?

(continued)

C. Where can you find employment in this job/career. For example, a mechanic might find employment at a car dealership; a privately- or corporate-owned repair shop; school district maintenance shops; local, state or federal governments; etc.

D. What are the estimated starting salaries for a person entering this job/career?

E. Prepare a works-cited list in MLA format that lists all the resources you used. You need to use a minimum of two sources. The works-cited list will receive a separate grade.

Assignment #3: Job Application Letter and Resume

See separate handout for specific requirements.

You need to complete BOTH of the following. Make it real, something you will use.

A. A job application letter. Find a job announcement in a local paper, or online. Print out the job announcement and turn it in with your letter of application.

B. Develop a resume. Create a resume based on your current education, job qualifications, and skill sets that qualify you for employment in your first career/job choice.

Assignment #4: Reflection

• Write a statement (one paragraph to one page) that analyzes the process you went through in obtaining the above information for Assignments 1–3.

• What worked for you?

• What didn't work for you?

• As a result of the research you have done, have you changed your thinking about what you intend to do? If yes, explain in what way(s).

• Did you find out anything that surprised you? Explain what surprised you. If you were not surprised or did not change your thinking, analyze how your research reinforced your commitment to your plans.

Additional Project Requirements:

1. Include a title page for the front of your project.

2. All work must be neatly typed. Missing information will cause point deductions. Grammar and mechanic errors will significantly lower the grade.

3. Turn in two complete copies of this assignment. One will go in a folder to be saved for your senior portfolio due in the spring. You'll have one section done. If you don't turn it in now, you will be responsible for providing this career packet in the spring.

4. Feel free to include in your career packet any brochures, photocopies of information, or other materials that you obtain that have helped you in your career search process.

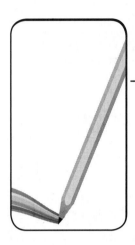

Appendix B

Blank Forms

Class Learning Profile

Nobody's Like Me

Student Self-Assessment and Reflections Form

Group Self-Reflection and Rating Rubric

Class Learning Profile

Goal:

Teacher: Subject: Standards:

Learning Element	Student's Strengths	Student's Needs	Student's Preferences/Interests
Learning "what"			
Learning "how"			
Learning "why"			

Source: Adapted from *Teaching Every Student in the Digital Age: Universal Design for Learning*, by David Rose and Anne Meyer, Alexandria, VA: ASCD. © 2002 by ASCD. Adapted with permission. Learn more about ASCD at www.ascd.org.

In *Teaching Transition Skills in Inclusive Schools* by Teresa Grossi, Ph.D., and Cassandra M. Cole, Ed.D.
(2013, Paul H. Brookes Publishing Co., Inc.)

Nobody's Like Me

Directions: Find some markers. Then, using symbols, pictures, or words, portray yourself by creatively/ artistically answering the following questions in the corresponding space on your body figure:

1. Where do you want your feet to take you?

2. What makes you really want to listen?

3. What is your favorite smell from childhood?

4. What is something you simply cannot stomach?

5. What can you see in yourself that others often cannot?

6. What do you have to say?

7. What do you recognize is above you?

8. What is a burden you shoulder?

9. What do you like to do with your hands?

10. What do you have your heart set on?

After responding to all the questions on your body figure, share what your symbols, pictures, and words mean with others in your small group (4 or 5). Knowing and being known is important to feelings of safety. Activities like this help us to know ourselves and one another better.

From Indiana Institute on Disability and Community (2012). Nobody's like me activity. Bloomington, IN: Author; reprinted by permission. In *Teaching Transition Skills in Inclusive Schools* by Teresa Grossi, Ph.D., and Cassandra M. Cole, Ed.D. (2013, Paul H. Brookes Publishing Co., Inc.)

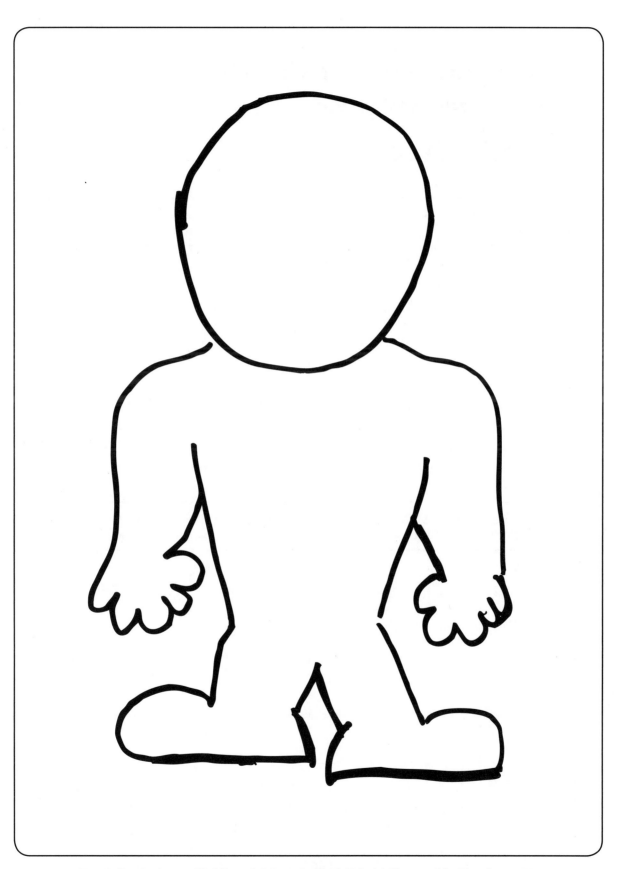

Student Self-Assessment and Reflections

Name _____   **Class** _____

Give a brief description of the project or activity you have completed.	What did you like about this project or activity? What were you able to do well?
What did you not like about this project or activity? What problems did you have? Why?	What did you learn about yourself? Include strengths, interests, preferences, and needs.

From Idaho Association of Teachers of Language and Culture (n.d.) Self-evaluation form for group work. Reprinted by permission. In *Teaching Transition Skills in Inclusive Schools* by Teresa Grossi, Ph.D., and Cassandra M. Cole, Ed.D. (2013, Paul H. Brookes Publishing Co., Inc.)

Group Self-Reflection and Rating Rubric

Your Name _____

Use this rubric to rate your group performance.

	Rarely	Sometimes	Often
All group members shared ideas			
All group members listened to and respected the ideas of others			
All group members were able to compromise and negotiate solutions			
All group members showed initiative in creating the group project			
All group members gathered the necessary information from appropriate resources			
All group members shared in the workload			

The two things I learned from this group project were:

1.

2.

The two things I would do differently when I work in a group.

1.

2.

Overall grade you would give yourself: (A+ - F) _____

Overall grade you would give the group: (A+ - F) _____

Overall grade you would give each peer: (A+ - F) _____

(A+ - F) _____

(A+ - F) _____

"Group Self-Reflection and Rating Rubric" adapted from Idaho Association of Teachers of Language and Culture (n.d.).
In *Teaching Transition Skills in Inclusive Schools* by Teresa Grossi, Ph.D., and Cassandra M. Cole, Ed.D.
(2013, Paul H. Brookes Publishing Co., Inc.)

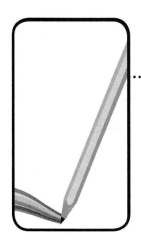

5

....

One Step Further

Supporting Students with Unique Needs

We know that all students can benefit from access to the general education curriculum and the unified system of transition services. Yet, there are some students who need additional internal and external supports. There are many resources addressing the issues of transition planning for students with higher support needs; this chapter is not intended to duplicate those resources but to provide some ideas and considerations for including students with more unique needs into our conceptual framework.

This chapter is intended for teachers who teach students who are taking the alternate state assessment, may or may not be on a diploma track, and may or may not have college as a postsecondary goal. These are students who need to have supplemental supports in place in order to be successful and those with unique needs that require more individualized and specialized instruction and transition services to supplement those described in the previous chapters. These students may be considered as Tier 3 in the RTI model and need an individualized curriculum. However, the core of the conceptual framework (quality instruction, academic rigor and standards, personalization, career exploration, and inclusive practices) is as important for this group of students as for all students.

QUALITY INSTRUCTION

Many of the concepts and principles of UDL described in Chapter 3 are applicable for students with higher support needs. Teachers should use multiple means of representation, multiple means of action and expression, and multiple means of engagement. Examples would include presenting information using different modalities, speech to text technologies, and visual and auditory cues; preteaching key concepts; using physical manipulatives; providing choice, visual schedules, and peer support; and using components of differentiated instruction.

There are some students who may need a greater degree of adaptation and accommodations to meet the academic requirements. Figure 5.1 highlights the nine ways to adapt, with special emphasis on three adaptations that are most appropriate for this group of students. As noted in Chapter 3, the first six adaptations are appropriate for all students. The last three (degree of participation, modified goals, and substitute curriculum) should be considered only after the first six are used. Knowing students well will assist teachers in making decisions about the types of accommodations needed.

Input	Output	Size
The instructional strategies used to facilitate student learning. *For example:* Using of videos, computer programs, field trips, and visual aides to support active learning.	The ways learners can demonstrate understanding and knowledge. *For example:* To demonstrate understanding, students write a song, tell a story, design a poster or brochure, perform an experiment	The length or portion of an assignment, demonstration or performance learners are expected to complete. *For example:* Reduce the length of report to be written or spoken, reduce the number of references needed or the number of problems to be solved.
Time	**Difficulty**	**Level of Support**
The flexible time needed for student learning. *For example:* Individualize a timeline for project completion, allow more time for test taking.	The varied skill levels, conceptual levels and processes involved in learning. *For example:* Provide calculators, tier the assignment so the outcome is the same but with varying degrees of concreteness and complexity.	The amount of assistance to the learner. *For example:* Student work in cooperative groups, or with peer buddies, mentors, cross-age tutors or paraeducators.
Degree of Participation	**Modified Goals**	**Substitute Curriculum**
The extent to which the learner is actively involved in the tasks. *For example:* In a student written, directed, and acted play, a student may play a part that has more physical action rather than numerous lines to memorize.	The adapted outcome expectations within the context of a general education curriculum. *For example:* In a written language activity, a student may focus more on writing some letters and copying words rather than composing whole sentences or paragraphs.	The significantly differentiated instruction and materials to meet a learner's identified goal. *For example:* In a foreign language class, a student may develop a play or script that uses both authentic language and cultural knowledge of a designated time period, rather than reading paragraphs or directions.

Figure 5.1. Nine types of adaptations. (From Cole, S., Horvath, B., Chapman, C., Deschenes, C., Ebeling, D.G., & Sprague, J. [2000]. *Adapting curriculum and instruction in inclusive classrooms: A teacher's desk reference.* [2nd ed.]. Bloomington, IN: Indiana Institute on Disability and Community, Indiana University; reprinted by permission.)

The use of technology in schools has increased dramatically and offers a promising tool for many students who require more intensive supports. There is little that cannot be done electronically. For example, daily planners, virtual online courses, web tools and apps, portfolios, online discussion forums, homework assignments, visual schedules, and text-to-speech can provide a spectrum of supports, from low to high tech, general to specific. Tablet computers, such as the iPad, Toshiba Thrive, and others, provide a great tool for students to use in a variety of ways. In many schools, these tablets are being used by all members of the school: teachers, administrators, and students. This makes it a natural way to adapt and support students who have greater learning and social challenges.

In Chapter 4, we discussed ways to get to know students and to use this information in transition planning and use of class profiles. For students with higher support needs, there are some unique details that need to be understood, documented and addressed in

> *The use of technology in schools has increased dramatically and offers a promising tool for many students who require more intensive supports.*

Many applications for mobile devices and tablet computers have recently been developed specifically for students with autism spectrum disorders and other disabilities. Examples of apps cover areas of communication, cognitive challenges, restrictive behavior and special interests, social challenges, sensory and motor challenges, and others. The Ohio Center for Autism and Low Incidence includes an extensive list of such apps on their website: http://www.ocali.org/up_archive_doc/Spectrum_Apps_ASD.pdf

order for a student to be able to access school and community environments. This information can be compiled in a class learning profile (see Chapter 4) to include students with high support needs in various general education classes. Using this information for transition planning may also help to identify the external supports that may be needed. Figure 5.2 shows an example of a profile of a student with higher support needs.

Many supports designed for students with more significant needs ultimately end up supporting other students in the school and become a part of the school culture. Designing supports that include strategies that are usable for a variety of students is important and follows the principles of universal design. For example, many students with autism spectrum disorders or similar disabilities benefit from visual supports. Figure 5.3 shows an example of inverted triangle that can serve as a visual support for all students or be tailored to an individual student. For use with an entire class, the five levels could indicate

1. Individual seat work

2. Partner work

3. Cooperative learning group

4. Whole-group instruction

5. Instruction in another setting (i.e., computer lab, media center)

A classroom teacher might post the triangle figure on the board or project it on the wall, with one level circled or clearly marked, to instruct all students as to what's expected of them during this work period. By using colors, differently sized levels, and numbers, students at just about any learning level will clearly understand what is expected of them.

Student Name: Emily King	**Date:** August 30, 2012
A Few Things About Emily	**Emily's Strengths, Abilities and Support Needs**
• Loves to be with peers and benefits from peer support (This year Sara and Amy are supporting her in the cafeteria and in science.) • Enjoys and participates in choir and music • May talk loudly when she gets excited • Swims in adaptive PE twice a week • Knows if someone doesn't like her—she avoids certain people • Has supportive parents who assist with AT device use at home • Has a dog named Sadie • Visits her grandmother once a month • Wants to be involved in extracurricular activities like musicals • Will be doing be doing inschool work experience this semester helping the office staff • Related services monitors (biweekly) • Needs more career exploration activities to help vision for the future	*Communication* Good receptive language; difficult to understand at times with expressive language; using AT device to supplement voice *Mobility* Limited ability to walk; occupational therapist monitors transfers *Personal Care (meal time, grooming, hygiene)* Needs help dressing after PE; needs assistance in restroom for transferring and at meal time *Vision/Hearing* Good *Manipulation* Good *Equipment* Motorized wheelchair: Maneuvers well; uses laptop computer *Health and Safety* Has had several surgeries; overall good health
Where to Find More Information	
• Medical file with school nurse and health plan attached to transition IEP with Ms. Held (along with academic performance)	

Figure 5.2. Student information profile. (From Ferguson, D.L., Ralph, G., Meyer, G., Lester, J., Droege, C., Guojonskottir, H., Sampson, N., & Williams, J. [2001]. *Designing personalized learning for every student.* Alexandria, VA: ASCD; adapted by permission.)

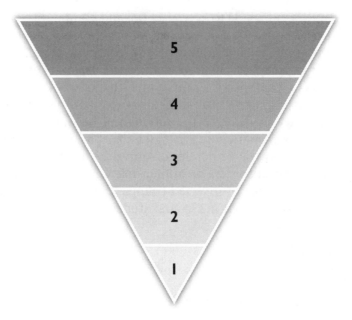

Figure 5.3. Inverted triangle for visual support.

This visual can be adapted for a variety of content area classes and purposes. The goal is for students to become more self-directed and independent, a critical transition skill.

There are many different types of visual supports that can be tailored for an individual student. As transition goals are addressed, it is important that the visual can be used in a variety of settings and adapted for future use in a work and living environments.

ACADEMIC RIGOR AND STANDARDS

In Chapter 3 we introduced the Common Core Standards, which many states have already adopted. The Common Core Standards support college and career readiness and should be considered along with standards specifically targeted to career readiness (State Career Cluster Initiative, 2008). This is also true for students with higher support needs. Courtade and Browder (2011) discussed the challenges educators face in determining ways to make state standards accessible to students who have higher support needs. For example, how can a student who can only recognize numbers access math concepts such as algebraic equations? Courtade and Browder offered four ways to generate ideas for creating access to standards. They include

- Select skills that promote overall English, language arts, and mathematics skills

- Focus on self-determination skills

- Use assistive technology to increase active independent responding

- Use real-life activities to give meaning to the academic concept (p. 33)

In their paper "What does 'College and Career Ready' Mean for Students with Significant Cognitive Disabilities?" Kearns, Kleinert, Harrison, et al. (2010) discussed the importance of the skill sets associated with the college- and career-ready standards represent important learning for these students. The authors provide five general goals to move students with high support needs closer to achieving those skills necessary to become "college and career ready."

1. Recognizing and developing communicative competence should be addressed for students with significant cognitive disabilities by the time they are in Kindergarten.

2. Fluency in reading, writing, and math are necessary for the pursuit of information whether used for lifelong learning, leisure, or vocational purposes.

3. Age-appropriate social skills and the ability to work effectively in small groups are essential for future educational as well as vocational pursuits.

4. Independent work behaviors, as well as assistance-seeking behavior, are critical for lifelong learning pursuits including vocational success.

5. Skills in accessing support systems are essential for long-term success. (pp. 24–25)

Academic rigor and high expectations should not be reserved for a select group of students but should be considered for all students. Often, for students with greater challenges, the temptation is to lower standards and expectations, when in fact this group of students needs to continually be challenged.

CAREER EXPLORATION

The instruction discussed in Chapter 3 and 4 are applicable to career technical education programs offered at career centers or vocational education programs. There are students who may not meet all the academic requirements of career tech programs. Yet, they can gain a variety of skill sets that would make them marketable in the workplace. For example, a student may not meet the competencies to become an auto mechanic but could learn specific skills to enable him or her to work in businesses that offer specialty services such as oil change, muffler repair, or detailing. In addition, these students may be able to work in parts stores and auto supply stores. Career-tech programs should have an inclusive philosophy, recognizing that all students can benefit from being a part of a career program.

Students also benefit from opportunities for community-based instruction and work experiences. Community-based instruction is a key element of effective secondary education and transition programs for students with higher support needs. For more extensive information about effective specialized instructional procedures, data collection strategies, and community-based instruction, please see *Evidence-Based Instructional Strategies for Transition* (Test, 2012).

A key element of a variety of community and work-based experiences is discovering who the student is and capturing it to include in the transition-planning process to inform future employment. This profile can be used when communicating with general educators to help get to know the student or to guide his or her career plans or job development activities. As described by Luecking (2009),

a positive personal profile is a practical way of "taking inventory" of an individual's attributes that will be relevant to identifying potential work experiences and jobs, as well as later job searches, job matches, job retention, and long-range career development. (p. 46)

The profile is a way of gathering information that will be helpful in transition planning as well as careers. The basic information that should be included in the profile is dreams and goals, interests, talents, skills, knowledge, learning style, values, positive personality traits, environmental preferences, dislikes, life and work experiences, support systems, specific challenges, creative solutions and accommodations, and creative possibilities. Figure 5.4 shows an example of how one local high school adapted and used Luecking's framework to develop student profiles for youth with higher support needs.

PERSONALIZATION

As we discussed in Chapter 3, personalization is the learning process in which schools help students access their own talents and aspirations. For students with higher support needs, teachers should use multiple sources of data to get to know their students. This includes mentors, person-centered planning approaches, various transition assessments tools, and a variety of experiences through community-based instruction (CBI) and community-based work experiences.

Person-centered planning, as discussed briefly in Chapter 4, is an effective transition planning approach, especially for individuals with higher support needs. It focuses on the capacities of the individual, not the deficits. It uses the process of discovery to identify the person's strengths, gifts, hopes, and preferences (PACER Center, 2004) Many students with higher support needs lack the experiences to determine what they like and don't like. Therefore, it is essential that a variety of experiences through inschool, community, and work-based learning are offered to help determine what works and doesn't work for the student as well as his or her interests and preferences. For students who don't communicate verbally, it is important for teachers, family members, job coaches, and others who know them well to be keen observers to help inform the planning process. Words and pictures can be used to represent transition goals or use of PowerPoint presentations, video clips, collages, or other electronic applications and programs with clip art can help communicate the student's information. Using the UDL principles, there are multiple means of representation, engagement, and expression that can be used for students.

Another mentor-type approach is the "Check & Connect" (Christenson, Thurlow, Sinclair et al., 2008), which is structured to enhance personal contact and opportunities to build positive and trusting relationships. It is a comprehensive intervention designed to enhance student engagement at school and learning for marginalized and disengaged students. Student levels of engagement (e.g., attendance, grades, suspensions) are "checked" regularly and used to guide the efforts of mentors (e.g., teachers, counselors, paraeducators or paraprofessionals, social workers, school psychologists, or community members) to increase and maintain students' "connection" with school. Over 20 years of research has shown increased attendance rates, persistence in school, accrual of credits, and school completion rates while a showing decrease in truancy, tardiness, behavioral referrals, and drop-out rates (see also http://www.checkandconnect.org/).

INCLUSIVE PROGRAM PRACTICES

Students with higher support needs benefit from learning and interacting alongside their peers. For students with disabilities the experience with peers can provide opportunities to improve communication skills, increase social interaction skills, increase academic skills, and build friendships. This provides avenues for students to more actively participate in

**High School South
Student Profile**

Name: ___Cayden___   Beginning date: _9.10.11___
Date of updates: 9.23.12; _____; _____; _____;

Interviews should occur with student, parents, teachers, and others who know the student well and be built upon over the years.

Dreams and Goals	**Talents, Skills, and Knowledge**
• Work in a competitive job with supports • Live in his own place with supports (supported-living services) • Have friends	• Can follow simple routines and activities • Can follow the sequence of a schedule • Good eye-hand coordination • Good physical abilities • Willing to try new activities • Can ride the city bus with minimal supports • Good computer skills • Can match letters to sounds • Can read one- to two-syllable words • Initiates communication with others • Good problem solving
Learning Styles and What Works • Works well 1:1 or in small group • Use of social stories • Structured learning environments • Structured teaching elements • Uses schedule to transition from one activity to another and understand his day • Visual supports	**Dislikes and What Does Not Work:** • Confined to a close or office space • Loud noises • People yelling or being "mean"
Interests and Values • Socializing • Being around people • Sports especially football and basketball	**Positive Personality Traits (including temperament)** • Very social • Likeable • Good problem-solver • Easy going in that will try new things • Likes to please
Environmental Preferences • Likes outdoors	**Life and Work Experiences** • Had in-classroom jobs in middle school
Specific Challenges • Physical aggression has decreased. • Self-help skills • Daily living skills • Self-slapping hands (easily redirected with visuals) • Most outings are 2:1 due to behaviors. • When frustrated or aggravated he will become physically aggressive (pulling clothes, grabbing wrists and head, self-abusive) and vocally loud (cries). • When denied a wanted activity or object, gets aggressive	**Support Needs, Support Systems, and Accommodations** • Visual supports • Redirecting • Visual schedules • Family is involved but wearing out • One older and one younger sister. • Aunts/uncles are also involved

Work Experiences, Ideas, and Possibilities to Explore
• Working in athletic department to be around other guys—possibly laundry and equipment cleaning
• Hands-on activities—landscaping

Other Experiences (community-based instruction, courses, extracurricular)
• Helping with football team
• Community-based instruction (CBI) will increase to twice a week.
• General education classes—art, physical education, and music; will explore helping with theater to build stage props

Figure 5.4. Student profile example. (From Luecking, R. [2009]. *The way to work: How to facilitate work experiences for youth in transition* [p. 57–58]. Baltimore, MD: Paul H. Brookes Publishing Co.; adapted by permission.)

the school community and have access to general education curriculum and activities. For students without disabilities, this interaction provides opportunities to embrace diversity, increase knowledge of human difference, and promote and advocate for inclusive communities. For students with and without disabilities there are improved social skills and self-esteem and simply the opportunity to make new friends (Bond-Brookes & Castagnera, 2010).

One vehicle to promote these skills is peer mentors or tutors. Peer tutors or mentors are high school students who receive elective credit to provide support to students with disabilities. Peer mentors or tutors are paired with students with disabilities to provide a wide range of supports based on student's individual needs such as support in academic and elective classes, and extracurricular, community-based, and school-wide activities.

Another program that is gaining momentum in high schools to support students with disabilities is the Best Buddies program. Best Buddies is a nonprofit organization dedicated to establishing a global volunteer movement that creates opportunities for one-to-one friendships, integrated employment, and leadership development for people with intellectual and developmental disabilities (IDD). Since 1993, Best Buddies High Schools has paired students with IDD in one-to-one friendships with high school students. Best Buddies has more than 900 high school chapters worldwide. For more information about Best Buddies, see www.bestbuddies.org.

Additionally, paraprofessionals play a critical role in the instruction and inclusion of students with higher support needs or significant disabilities. Paraprofessionals are hired to support students with disabilities receiving special education services. Although paraprofessionals have varied roles, they are vital to promoting inclusionary practices and advocating with students with disabilities. It is important that paraprofessionals have the necessary training and supervision and that they get to know their students well (Causton-Theoharis, 2009). Part of the training component for paraprofessionals is to ensure that their support and role does not create overreliance and dependency on the part of the student and family.

Paraprofessionals are hired to support students with disabilities receiving special education services. Although paraprofessionals have varied roles, they are vital to promoting inclusionary practices and advocating with students with disabilities.

INTERNAL AND EXTERNAL SUPPORTS

Schools are being asked to respond to the increased social and emotional needs of students that often mirror the changes in society. There are many students, with and without disabilities, who struggle with poverty, family dynamics, sexual orientation, community or domestic violence, bullying, and peer pressures. Schools must rely on both internal and external support systems to address student needs and prepare all students for life after high school.

Internally, many schools have created support groups led by school social workers and counselors. These groups provide students with an avenue to openly talk about their situations and learn coping strategies to manage their emotions. Schools may also partner with community agencies to create full service schools. Full-service community schools, as defined by the Coalition for Community Schools are "both a place and a set of partnerships between the school and other community resources" (Campbell-Allen, Pena Aekta Shah, Sullender, & Zazove, 2009, p.1). In this type of school, the school encourages coordination with community-based organizations, nonprofit organizations, and other private or public entities. For example, mental health services are provided within the school building and during the school day. Also, these services are expanding to support the family and community during non-school hours. (Campbell-Allen, et al., 2009).

Providing supports for students with unique needs requires schools to be open to flexible schedules. There are students who can benefit from a partial school day or who may not be able to manage a bell-to-bell routine. School staff may, on an individual basis, need to create alternative schedules and learning environments to meet student needs. For example, a student who may have high anxiety in large group settings may do well taking some portion or all of a course online. There may also be students whose school day would include treatment through a local mental health center.

SUMMARY

This book has focused primarily on students who are receiving a diploma, and most of the information presented in earlier chapters is applicable to all students. Yet, we acknowledge that there are students whose unique needs will require additional considerations and supports. Even as these students receive additional support and more individualized approaches, such as the considerations highlighted in this chapter, the process of planning and providing transition services for them still fits within the unified framework presented throughout this book. Students with unique support needs may still benefit from many of the practices in the universal level outlined earlier; the key, as always, is that specialized services supplement, not supplant, the instruction, planning, and support that is available to all students.

Online communities can be informative and supportive resources for teenagers and young adults with mental health challenges. Voices4Hope (http://www.voices4hope.net/) is one such site, funded by a federal grant, offering a place where young people can talk to each other and get reliable information about available services.

For many students with multiple disabilities, necessary related services such as speech-language, physical, and occupational therapy can provide services and consultation in various integrated settings where the student is, rather than pulling the student out. Related services are important to help identify what external supports the student will need after high school. For example, the adaptations used in school provided by an occupational therapist can help a student in the workplace.

Additional disability-specific external supports are often required for students with higher support needs to make the transition from high school to adult life. These agencies can include adult service providers to support employment, Vocational Rehabilitation Services, Developmental Disabilities Services, Mental Health, Medicaid, transportation, residential providers, and advocacy groups. It is important for educators to know their state and local resources to help ensure a seamless transition.

Finally, as the student reaches high school or adolescence and begins the transition process, families are faced with a variety of decisions and support needs. Educators must support families to help prepare for life after high school, identify the high school experiences that will assist the student (and families) to reaching the postschool goals, and make connections with the external supports, including disability-specific supports.

FOR FURTHER INFORMATION

Supporting Transition for Students with High Needs

Clark, H., & Unruh, D. (2009). *Transition of youth and young adults with emotional or behavioral difficulties.* Baltimore, MD: Paul H. Brookes Publishing Co.

Guidance on supporting young people with mental health issues as they transition to adulthood

McDonnell, J., & Hardman, M. (2010). *Successful transition programs: Pathways for students with intellectual and developmental disabilities.* Thousand Oaks, CA: Sage Publications.

Presents systemat ic approaches for planning for and supporting transition

Wehman, P., Datlow Smith, M., & Schall, C. (2009). *Autism and transition to adulthood.* Baltimore, MD: Paul H. Brookes Publishing Co.

Specific guidance for meeting the needs of young people with autism and addressing highly individualized transition planning

Articles and suggestions of numerous resources for supporting individuals with autism spectrum disorders

Courtade, G., & Browder, D. (2011) *Aligning IEPS to the Common Core State Standards for Moderate and Severe Disabilities.* Verona, WI: Attainment Company.

Framework for aligning state standards for students with higher support needs community-based instruction, effective instructional strategies and work-based learning

Test, D. (2012). *Evidence-based instructional strategies for transition.* Baltimore, MD: Paul H. Brookes Publishing Co.

Framework and examples of structured lesson plans to teach transition skills to students with moderate and severe disabilities

Luecking, R. (2009). *The way to work: How to facilitate work experiences for youth in transition.* Baltimore, MD: Paul H. Brookes Publishing Co.

Practical guide for establishing internships and other work experiences for students with disabilities

Person-centered planning: A tool for transition planning (2004). PACER Center, Parent Brief. Minneapolis, MN

Wehman, P., Inge, K., Revell, W.G., & Brooke, V.A. (2007). *Real work for real pay: Inclusive employment for people with disabilities.* Baltimore, MD: Paul H. Brookes Publishing Co.

Strategies employers, job coaches, and schools can use to ensure people with disabilities have full opportunities in real jobs

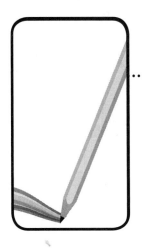

Appendix A
Student Profile

Name:_____   Beginning date: _____

Date of updates: _____; _____; _____; _____;

Interviews should be with student, parents, teachers, and others who know the student well and should be built upon over the years.

Dreams and Goals:	Talents, Skills, and Knowledge:
Learning Styles and What Works:	**Dislikes and What Does Not Work:**
Interests and Values:	**Positive Personality Traits (including temperament):**
Environmental Preferences:	**Life and Work Experiences:**

From Luecking, R. (2009). *The way to work: How to facilitate work experiences for youth in transition* (pp. 57–62). Baltimore, MD: Paul H. Brookes Publishing Co.; adapted by permission. In *Teaching Transition Skills in Inclusive Schools* by Teresa Grossi, Ph.D., and Cassandra M. Cole, Ed.D. (2013 by Paul H. Brookes Publishing Co., Inc.)

Specific Challenges:	Support Needs, Support Systems, and Accommodations:

Work Experiences, Ideas, and Possibilities to Explore:

Other Experiences (CBI, courses, extracurricular):

Student Profile Explanations and Possible Interview Questions

Dreams and goals—What are the student's aspirations? Try to find a connection between his or her aspirations and some type of work experience. Remember, it's about helping the student to make an informed decision (not professionals deciding for them).

Talents, skills, and knowledge—What are natural gifts, things the student has a knack for? Include past formal or informal assessments. What do people compliment him or her about? Think about academic, money skills, time, artistic, manual, physical, and social skills.

Learning styles—What instruction yields the best learning for the student? How does the student best learn a new task? What works for this student?

Interests—Think about hobbies and leisure or what type of experiences may need to occur to determine some interests for the student. How can you encourage the student and/or family to take some risks to try new things or try things that may be beyond the limitations to expand skills and interests.

Values—These are important when determining the type of work and the type of company the student will want to work for. Remember the family and cultural views.

Positive personality traits—How do people describe the student? Friendly, focused, detail oriented, honest, nice smile, sense of humor, lots of energy. Stay positive!

Environmental preferences—Does the student prefer and work best under specific conditions such as routine or varied tasks? Fast-paced environments where things change rapidly? Indoors or outdoors? Does he or she prefer quiet setting or can the student handle distractions? Are people present for support or supervision? Is the environment relaxed and flexible, or does it have very strict rules?

Dislikes—Ask the student, "What is the job or setting do you not want to do?" Think about things that don't work for this student, such as getting dirty, loud noises, sitting for long periods of time, people talking loudly, etc. What does not work for this student? Are there situations that should be avoided? Are there particular activities the student does not like to do?

From Luecking, R. (2009). *The way to work: How to facilitate work experiences for youth in transition* (pp. 57–62). Baltimore, MD: Paul H. Brookes Publishing Co.; adapted by permission. In *Teaching Transition Skills in Inclusive Schools* by Teresa Grossi, Ph.D., and Cassandra M. Cole, Ed.D. (2013 by Paul H. Brookes Publishing Co., Inc.)

Life and work experiences—For students with little or no work experiences, are there some life experiences that could be translated into useful skills in the workplace, such as household chores, babysitting, or volunteering at church? For students who have had some work experiences, list the setting and type of work such as a school job—delivering mail; office setting—data entry. How is the student getting around in the community now?

Support system—Are there people around the student who can provide support, encouragement, and/or resources for planning, developing, and assisting in the work experience? Think about people who can help make employer connections for the student. This should include both family/friends and paid professionals.

Specific challenges—These include low reading/math ability, grooming/hygiene, behavioral, assistive technology, social skills (appropriate conversations), transportation, home environments, substance abuse, etc.

Support needs and accommodations—This would be the solutions to the specific challenges or barriers, such as picture prompts for predictability, a coworker serving as a mentor, a neighbor providing transportation, etc. What are the accommodations that are being provided in school now that can be used on the work site?

Possibilities and ideas—This is the time to brainstorm potential sites and specific types of work. The goal is to build upon the experiences and what is learned about the student from each of them to help lead to a paid job.

From Luecking, R. (2009). *The way to work: How to facilitate work experiences for youth in transition* (pp. 57–62). Baltimore, MD: Paul H. Brookes Publishing Co.; adapted by permission. In *Teaching Transition Skills in Inclusive Schools* by Teresa Grossi, Ph.D., and Cassandra M. Cole, Ed.D. (2013 by Paul H. Brookes Publishing Co., Inc.)

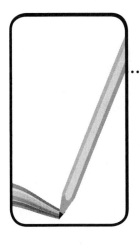

References

Achieve (2004). *The Expectations Gap: A 50 state review of high school graduation requirements.* Retrieved from http://www.achieve.org/files/coursetaking.pdf

Barclay, J., Holmes, S., Elmore, D., Dupuis, B., Lewis, V., & Shaha, S.H. (2006). Closing the gap: Inclusion for maximizing the impact of exceptional student education programs. *Proceedings of the International Conference on Education.* Honolulu, HI. 4, 229.

Benson, B.P, & Barnett, S.P. (2005). *Student-led conferencing: Using showcase portfolios.* Thousand Oaks, CA: Corwin Press.

Bond-Brookes, R., & Castagnera, E. (2010). *Peer tutoring and support: Making inclusive education work.* Colorado Springs, CO: PEAK Parent Center, Inc.

Boyer, E.L. (1983). *High school: A report on secondary education in America.* The Carnegie Foundation for the Advancement of Teaching. New York, NY: Harper and Row.

Breaking Ranks II: Strategies for leading high school reform (2004). National Association of Secondary High School Principals. Reston, VA.

Brolin, D.E. (1995). *Career education: A functional life skills approach* (3rd ed.). Englewood Cliffs, NJ: Prentice-Hall, Inc.

Brophy J., & Good, T. (1986). Teacher behavior and student achievement. In M.C. Wittrock (ed.), *Handbook of research on teaching* (3rd ed.). New York, NY: McMillan.

Burrello, L., Lashley, C., & Beatty, E. (2001). *Educating all students together: How school leaders create unified systems.* Thousand Oaks, CA: Corwin Press.

Campbell-Allen, R., Pena Aekta Shah, M., Sullender, R., & Zazove, R. (2009). *Full-Service schools policy review and recommendations.* Boston, MA: Harvard School of Education.

Carroll, J. (1963). A model of school learning. *Teachers College Record, 64,* 723–733.

Carroll, J.B. (1989). The Carroll model: A 25-Year retrospective and prospective view, *Educational Researcher, 18* (1) 26–31

Causton-Theoharis, J. (2009). *The paraprofessional's handbook for effective support in inclusive classrooms.* Baltimore, MD: Paul H. Brookes Publishing Co.

Center for Applied Special Technology. (2008). *Universal design for learning guidelines version 2.0.* Wakefield, MA: Author.

Center on Education and the Workforce. (2010). *Help wanted: Projections of jobs and education requirements through 2018.* Washington, DC: University of Georgetown, Center on Education and the Workforce. Retrieved from http://www9.georgetown.edu/grad/gppi/hpi/cew/pdfs/FullReport.pdf

Center on Education and Lifelong Learning at Indiana Institute on Disability and Community (2012). In-common quilt. Bloomington, IN: Author. Retrieved from http://www.iidc.indiana.edu/?pageId=3470

Christenson, S.L., Thurlow, M.L., Sinclair, M.F., Lehr, C.A., Kaibel, C.M., Reschly, A.L., Mavis, A., & Pohl, A. (2008). *Check & connect: A comprehensive student engagement intervention manual.* Minneapolis, MN: Institute on Community Integration. http://www.checkandconnect.org/

Clark, J.H. (2003). *Changing systems to personalize learning: Introduction to the personalization workshops.* Providence, RI: Education Alliance at Brown University.

Clark, H., & Unruh, D. (2009). *Transition of youth and young adults with emotional or behavioral difficulties.* Baltimore, MD: Paul H. Brookes Publishing Co

Cole, C., & McLeskey, J. (1997). Secondary inclusion programs for students with mild disabilities. *Focus on Exceptional Children, 29,* 1–15.

Cole, C., Waldron, N., & Madj, C. (2004). The academic progress of students across inclusive and traditional settings. *Mental Retardation, 42*(2), pp. 136–144

Cole, S., Horvath, B, Chapman, C., Deschenes, Ebeling, D., & Sprague, J. (2000). *Adapting curriculum and instruction in inclusive classrooms: A teacher's desk reference.* (2nd ed.). Bloomington, IN: Indiana Institute on Disability and Community, Indiana University.

Common Core Standards. (2010). Retrieved from http://www.corestandards.org/articles/8-national-governors-association-and-state-education-chiefs-launch-common-state-academic-standards

Courtade, G., & Browder, D. (2011) *Aligning IEPS to the Common Core State Standards for Moderate and Severe Disabilities.* Verona, WI: Attainment Company.

Dagget, W. (2005). *Achieving academic excellence through rigor and relevance.* Rexford, NY: International Center for Leadership in Education.

Darling-Hammond, L., & Sykes, G. (1999). *Teaching as the learning profession: A handbook of policy and practice.* San Francisco, CA: Jossey-Bass.

Dean, C., Hubbell, E.R., Pitler, H., & Stone, B.J. (2012). *Classroom instruction that works: Research-based strategies for increasing student achievement.* (2nd ed.). Alexandria, VA: Association for Supervision and Curriculum Development.

Deshler, D.D., & Schumaker, J. *(Eds.). (2006). Teaching adolescents with disabilities: Accessing the general education curriculum.* Thousand Oaks , CA : Corwin.

DeRoche, E.F., & Williams, M.M. (2001). *Educating hearts and minds: A comprehensive character education framework.* (2nd ed.). Thousand Oaks, CA: Corwin.

Division of Career Development and Transition. Reston, VA: Council for Exceptional Children

Education for All Handicapped Children Act of 1975, Pub. L. No. 94-142, 20 U.S.C. §§ 1400 et seq.

Franker, K. (2007). Collaboration rubric. Menomonie, WI: University of Wisconsin, Stout. Retrieved from http://www2.uwstout.edu/content/profdev/rubrics/secondary teamworkrubric.html

Fullan, M., Hill, P., & Crevole, C. (2006). *Breakthrough.* Thousand Oaks, CA: Corwin.

Given, B.K. (2002). *Teaching to the brain's natural learning systems.* Alexandria, VA: Association for Supervision and Curriculum Development.

Gravois, T.A., Knotek, S., & Babinski, L.M. (2002). Educating practitioners as consultants: Development and implementation of instructional consultation team consortium. *Journal of Educational and Psychological Consultation, 13,* 113–132.

Greenan, S., Powers, L.E., & Lopez-Vasquez, A. (2006). Barriers against and strategies for promoting involvement of culturally diverse parents in school-based transition planning. *Journal for Vocational Special Needs Education, 27*(3), 4–14.

Greene, G. (2011). *Transition planning for culturally and linguistically diverse youth.* Baltimore, MD: Paul H. Brookes Publishing Co.

Greene, G. (2009). Best practices in transition. In C. Kochhar-Bryant & G. Greene. *Pathways to successful transition for youth with disabilities: A developmental process.* (2nd ed.). Upper Saddle River, NJ: Pearson Education, Inc.

Grossi, T., & Cole, C. (2007). *Postschool outcomes of students with disabilities across inclusive and traditional settings.* Unpublished manuscript, Indiana University, Bloomington, Indiana.

Henderson, A.T., & Mapp, K.L. (2002). *A new wave of evidence: The impact of school, family, and community connections on student achievement.* Austin, TX: Southwest Education Development Laboratory. Retrieved from www.sedl.org/connections/resources/evidence.pdf

Henderson, A.T. (2007, March). *NCLB reauthorization: Effective strategies for engaging parents and communities in schools.* Testimony to the U.S. Senate Committee on Health, Education, Labor, and Pensions on March 28, 2007. Published

Hitchcock, C., Meyer, A.M., Rose, D., & Jackson, J. (2002). *Access to, participation, and progress in the general education curriculum* [Technical brief]. Peabody, MA: National Center on Accessing the General Curriculum.

Hoover, J.J., & Patton, J.R. (2005). *Curriculum adaptations for students with learning and behavior problems: Differentiating instruction to meet diverse needs.* (3rd ed.). Austin, TX: PRO-ED.

Idaho Association of Teachers of Language and Culture (n.d.) Self-evaluation form for group work. Retrieved from www.iatlc.org/downloads/Peer%20and%20self%20evaluation.doc

Indiana Institute on Disability and Community (2012). Nobody's like me activity and figure. Bloomington, IN: Author. Retrieved from http://www.iidc.indiana.edu/?pageId=3470

Individuals with Disabilities Education Act (IDEA) of 1990, PL 101-476, 20 U.S.C. §§ 1400 *et seq.*

Individuals with Disabilities Education Act Amendments (IDEA) of 1997, PL 105-17, 20 U.S.C. §§ 1400 *et seq.*

Individuals with Disabilities Education Improvement Act (IDEA) of 2004, PL 108-446, 20 U.S.C. §§ 1400 *et seq.*

Johnson, D.R., Thurlow, M.L., & Stout, K.E. (2007). *Revisiting graduation requirements and diploma options for youth with disabilities: A national study* [Technical report 49]. Minneapolis, MN: University of Minnesota, National Center on Educational Outcomes.

Kendrick, M. (2000). When people matter more than systems. Keynote Presentation for the Conference "The Promise of Opportunity," Albany, NY, March 27–28, 2000.

Kern, L., Bambara, L., & Fogt, J. (2002). Class-wide curricular modification to improve the behavior of students with emotional or behavioral disorders. *Behavioral Disorders, 27*(4), 317–326.

Kochhar-Bryant, C., & Bassett, D. (2003). *Aligning transition and standards-based education: Issues and strategies.* Arlington, VA: Council for Exceptional Children.

Kochhar-Bryant, C., & Greene, G. (2009). *Pathways to successful transition for youth with disabilities: A developmental process.* (2nd ed.). Upper Saddle River, NJ: Pearson Education, Inc

Kohler, P. (1998). Implementing a transition perspective of education: A comprehensive approach to planning and delivering secondary education and transition services. In F.R. Rusch & J. Chadsey (Eds.), *High school and beyond: Transition from school to work* (pp. 179–205). Belmont, CA: Wadsworth.

Kristin, S. (2005). Effective high school reform: Research and policy that works. Washington, DC: National Conference of State Legislators

Luecking, R. (2009). *The way to work: How to facilitate work experiences for youth in transition* (p. 57). Baltimore, MD: Paul H. Brookes Publishing Co.

Marzano, R.J. (2003). *What works in schools: Translating research into action.* Alexandria, VA: Association for Supervision and Curriculum Development.

McDonnell, J., & Hardman, M. (2010). *Successful transition programs: Pathways for students with intellectual and developmental disabilities.* Thousand Oaks, CA: Sage Publications.

McGrath, D. (2009). *Effective goal process: A training module for educators.* Indianapolis, IN: Indiana Department of Education.

McLeskey, J., & Waldron, N. (2000). *Inclusive schools in action: Making differences ordinary.* Alexandria, VA: Association for Supervision and Curriculum Development.

McNulty, R.J., & Quaglia, R.J. (2007). Rigor, relevance and relationships. *School Administrator,* (64)8. American Association of School Administrators.

Me! Lessons for teaching self-awareness and self-advocacy. Retrieved from http://www.ou.edu/content/education/centers-and-partnerships/zarrow/trasition-education-materials/me-lessons-for-teaching-self-awareness-and-self-advocacy.html

Mount, B., & Zwernik, K. (1994). *Making futures happen: A manual for facilitators of personal futures planning.* St. Paul: Minnesota Governor's Council on Developmental Disabilities.

National Center on Secondary Education and Transition. (2003). *A National leadership summit on improving results for youth: State priorities and needs for assistance.* Retrieved from the National Center on Secondary Education and Transition website: http://www.ncset.org/summit03/NCSET Summit03findings.pdf

National Commission on Excellence in Education. (1983). *A nation at risk: The imperative for educational reform.* Washington DC: U.S. Government Printing Office.

National Conference of State Legislators. *Improving high schools through rigor, relevance and relationships.* Retrieved from http://www.ncsl.org/default.aspx?tabid=12879

National Dissemination Center for Children with Disabilities (2010). *Supports, modifications, and accommodations for students.* Retrieved from http://nichcy.org/schoolage/accommodations#part1

National Governors Association Center for Best Practices and the Council of Chief State School Officers. (2010a). *Common core state standards initiative.* Retrieved from http://www.corestandards.org/articles/8-national-governors-association-and-state-education-chiefs-launch-common-state-academic-standards

National Governors Association Center for Best Practices and the Council of Chief State School Officers. (2010b). *On the road to implementation: Achieving the promise of the common core state standards.* Retrieved from http://www.achieve.org/files/FINAL-CCSSImplementationGuide.pdf

National Response to Intervention Center. (2012). http://www.rti4success.org/.

National Secondary Transition Technical Assistance Center. (2008). *Team planning tool for improving transition education and services.* Charlotte, NC: Author.

National Secondary Transition Technical Assistance Center. (2011). *Evidence-based practices and lesson starter library.* Charlotte, NC: Author. Retrieved from www.nsttac.org

Newman, L., Wagner, M., Cameto, R., Knokey, A.M., & Shaver, D. (2010). *Comparisons across time of the outcomes of youth with disabilities up to 4 years after high school. A report from the National Longitudinal Transition Study (NLTS) and the National Longitudinal Transition Study-2 (NLTS-2).* Menlo Park, CA: SRI International.

Newman, L., Wagner, M., Huang, T., Shaver, D., Knokey, A.-M., Yu, J., Contreras, E., Ferguson, K., Greene, S., Nagle, K., & Cameto, R. (2011). *Secondary school programs and performance of students with disabilities. A special topic report of findings from the National Longitudinal Transition Study-2 (NLTS-2)* (NCSER 2012-3000). U.S. Department of Education. Washington, DC: National Center for Special Education Research. Menlo Park, CA: SRI International. Retrieved from www.nlts2.org/reports/2011_11/nlts2_report_2011_11_complete.pdf

No Child Left Behind Act of 2001, PL 107-110, 115 Stat. 1425, 20 U.S.C. §§ 6301 et seq.

Obama, B. (2009, February). Address to a Joint Session of Congress on February 24, 2009. Retrieved from http://www.whitehouse.gov/the_press_office/Remarks-of-President-Barack-Obama-Address-to-Joint-Session-of-Congress/

O'Brien, C., & O'Brien, J. (2000).*The origins of person-centered planning: A community of practice perspective.* Syracuse, NY: Syracuse University, Center on Human Policy.

O*Net Online, U.S. Department of Labor, Employment & Training Administration, http://www.onetonline.org/

PACER and the National Center on Secondary Education and Transition. (2004). *Person-centered planning: A tool for transition.* Retrieved from http://www.pacer.org/publications/parentbriefs/ParentBrief_Feb04.pdf

Palmer, S. (2010). Self-determination: A life-span perspective. *Focus on Exceptional Children, 42*(6), 1–16.

Phelps, L.A., & Hanley-Maxwell, C. (1997). School-to-work transitions for youth with disabilities: A review of outcomes and practices. *Review of Educational Research, 67,* 197–226.

Rea, P., McLaughlin, V., & Walther-Thomas, C. (2002). Outcomes for students with learning disabilities in inclusive and pull out programs. *Exceptional Children, 68*(2), 203–222.

Rennie Center for Education Research & Policy. (2011). *Student learning plans: Supporting every student's transition to college and career.* Cambridge, MA: Rennie Center for Education Research and Policy.

Rose, D.H., & Meyer, A. (2002). *Teaching every student in the digital age: Universal design for learning.* Alexandria, VA: Association for Supervision and Curriculum Development.

Sailor, W. (2002). Testimony from President's Commission on Excellence in Special Education: Research Agenda Task Force. Nashville, TN.

Sanders, W. L., & Horn, S. P. (1994). The Tennessee Value-Added Assessment System (TVAAS) Mixed model methodology in educational assessment. *Journal of Personnel Evaluation in Education, 8*(1), 299–311.

Senge, P. (2006). *The fifth discipline: The art and practice of the learning organization.* New York, NY: Doubleday.

Sitlington, P.L., & Clark, G.M. (2006). *Transition education and services for students with disabilities* (4th ed.). Boston, MA: Allyn & Bacon.

Sitlington, P.L., Neubert, D.A., & Leconte, P.J. (1997). Transition assessment: The position of the division of career development and transition. *Career Development for Exceptional Individuals, 20*(1), 69–79.

Sitlington, P.L., Neubert, D.A., Begun, W.H., Lombard, R.C., and LeConte, P.J., (2007). *Assess for Success: A Practitioner's Handbook on Transition Assessment,* (2nd ed.) Thousand Oaks, CA: Corwin Press;

Sizer, T. (1984). *Horace's compromise. The dilemma of the American high school.* Boston, MA: Houghton Mifflin.

Sizer, T. (2004a). *The red pencil: Convictions from experience in education.* New Haven, CT: Yale University Press

Sizer, T. (2004b). Forward in *Breaking ranks II: Strategies for leading high school reform.* Reston, VA: National Association of Secondary High School Principals.

Slavin, R. (1995). A model of effective instruction. *The Educational Forum, 59,* 166–176.

State Career Cluster Initiative, (2008). National Association of State Directors of Career Technical Education Consortium. MD: Silver Springs (www.careertech.org).

Student-directed transition planning lesson materials. Retrieved from http://www.ou.edu/content/education/centers-and-partnerships/zarrow/transition-education-materials/student-directed-transition-planning.html

Teachnology. (2012). What is inquiry based learning? Retrieved from http://www.teach-nology.com/current trends/inquiry/

Test, D. (2012). *Evidence-based instructional strategies for transition.* Baltimore, MD: Paul H. Brookes Publishing Co.

Thoma, C.A., Bartholomew, C.C., & Scott, L.A. (2009). *Universal design for transition: A roadmap for planning and instruction.* Baltimore, MD: Paul H. Brookes Publishing Co.

Tomlinson, C. (1999). *The differentiated classroom: Responding to the needs of all learners.* Alexandria, VA: Association for Supervision and Curriculum Development.

Tomlinson, C.A. (2008). *How to differentiate instruction in mixed ability classrooms.* (2nd ed.). Alexandria, VA: Association for Supervision and Curriculum Development.

Tomlinson, C.A., Brimijoin, K., & Narvaez, L. (2008). The differentiated school: Making revolutionary changes in teaching and learning. Alexandria, VA: Association for Supervision and Curriculum Development.

Tomlinson, C.A., & Eidson, C.C. (2003). *Differentiation in practice: A resource guide for differentiating curriculum.* Alexandria, VA: Association for Supervision and Curriculum Development.

Tomlinson, C., & McTighe, J. (2006). *Integrating differentiated instruction and understanding by design: Connecting content and kids.* Alexandria, VA: Association for Supervision and Curriculum Development.

University of California at Berkeley Division of Student Affairs (n.d.). Name tag match maker. Berkeley, CA: Author. Retrieved from http://students.berkeley.edu/files/osl/Student_Orgs/Team_Builders/Name%20Tag%20Match%20Maker.pdf

Vygotsky, L.S. (1978). *Mind in society: The development of higher psychological processes.* Oxford, England: Harvard University Press.

Wagner, T. (2008).*The global achievement gap: Why even our best schools don't teach the new survival skills our children need—and what we can do about it.* New York, NY: Basic Books.

Waldron, N., & McLeskey, J. (1998). The effects of an inclusive school program on students with mild and severe learning disabilities. *Exceptional Children, 64,* 395–405.

Wehman, P. (2011). *Essentials of transition planning.* Baltimore, MD: Paul H. Brookes Publishing Co.

Wehman, P., Datlow Smith, M., & Schall, C. (2009). *Autism and transition to adulthood.* Baltimore, MD: Paul H. Brookes Publishing Co

Wehman, P., Inge, K., Revell, W.G., & Brooke, V.A. (2007). *Real work for real pay: Inclusive employment for people with disabilities.* Baltimore, MD: Paul H. Brookes Publishing Co.

Willis, J. (2008). *Preparing ALL Youth for Academic and Career Readiness.* Washington, DC: National Collaborative on Workforce and Disability for Youth, Institute for Educational Leadership.

Wright, S.P., L., Horn, S.P., & Sanders, W. L. (1997). Teacher and Classroom Context Effects on Student Achievement: Implications for Teacher Evaluation. *Journal of Personnel Evaluation in Education* 11: 57–67

Yonezawa, S., McClure, L., & Jones, M. (2012). *Personalization in schools: Students at the center.* Washington, DC: Jobs for the Future.

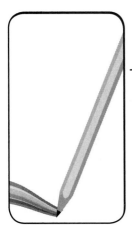

Index

Page references followed by *f* indicate figures; those followed by *t* indicate tables.

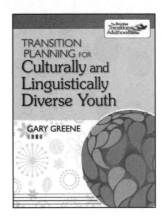